Returning to Holiness

A Personal and Churchwide Journey to Revival

A Biblical Guide to Daily Cleansing and Churchwide Solemn Assemblies

Dr. Gregory R. Frizzell

Returning to Holiness
ISBN 0-9665424-7-9

Copyright © 2000 by Gregory R. Frizzell
Edited by K N Rowland
Cover Design: S Faithe Finley
Published by The Master Design
  in cooperation with Master Design Ministries
PO Box 17865
Memphis, TN 38187-0865
Info@masterdesign.org
www.masterdesign.org

Unless otherwise noted, Scripture quotations are from the KING JAMES VERSION AV of the Bible © 1973, Thomas Nelson, Inc., Publishers.

Printed by Bethany Press International in the USA.

JJ

Other Books by Gregory R. Frizzell

- Prayer Evangelism for the Local Church: *"One Church's Miraculous Story of Blessing and Deliverance"*
- Local Associations and United Prayer: *Keys to the Coming Revival*
- How to Develop a Powerful Prayer Life
- Biblical Patterns for Powerful Church Prayer Meetings
- Statewide Prayer Strategies: *"Biblical Patterns for Spiritual Awakening"*
- A Five Year Associational Vision Based on 2 Chronicles 7:14
- National Strategies for Powerful United Prayer
- Pastors' Prayer Meetings: *"Journey to Areawide Revival"*
- Training Deacons for Crisis Counseling
- How to Develop an Evangelistic Church Prayer Ministry

Church and Areawide Conferences by Gregory R. Frizzell

- Developing a Powerful Prayer Life
- Developing Evangelistic Church Prayer Ministries
- Developing Associational and Statewide Prayer Strategies
- Developing an Historic and Biblical Vision for a Modern Great Awakening
- Church and Citywide Solemn Assemblies
- Biblical Patterns for Spiritual Warfare

Table of Contents

Foreword

If there was ever a time in the history of the church when the Body of Christ needed purifying, it is at the beginning of the twenty-first century. God wants His church to be a glorious Bride in the approaching wedding – the celestial wedding of the church with her great Bridegroom, the Lord Jesus Christ. Yet today, the church is characterized by indifference, halfhearted commitment, and even immorality among its members and leaders, both in gross and in small, seemingly undetectable forms. We desperately need to pay serious attention to our work in readying the Body of Christ.

Dr. Greg Frizzell has given every believer and pastor a tool for doing that most important of all works – purifying the church at this crucial time in her history. The one thing I have personally known of Dr. Frizzell over many years is his unwavering seriousness of purpose. That is what this work can and will inculcate in those who read it – they will become serious about their personal purity and that of their local church.

I urge every pastor to work his way carefully through the seven categories of sin and to answer for themselves personally the questions asked. They should ask their entire congregations to embrace this same process of examination and cleansing. Churches and church members are not Spirit-filled because they are ignorant of the areas of sin which prevent the Spirit from working totally in churches and individual lives. This book covers many areas of sinful behavior that exist because our people are ignorant of the terrible and wonderful demands of a Holy God. I myself have taught for many years on brokenness in our lives in order to know the fullness of God in our lives. This book has one of the finest discussions of brokenness that I have found. Brokenness is a rare concept in evangelical writings and Dr.

Frizzell has presented it fully and effectively.

I hope pastors, denominational leaders and every believer will take seriously God's intention to sanctify the church, as presented by Greg Frizzell in this important work. We as individuals and as assemblies of believers need it very much.

T. W. Hunt

Introduction

"Holiness — The Dawning of the Next Great Awakening!"

I have never sensed greater excitement or urgency than with God's assignment to write this book. Though I have taught this material for many years, God's leading to write it came with incredible suddenness. So great was the urgency, that the bulk of this work was actually completed in about ten days. Since I am normally not a fast writer, this signaled a most unusual moving of God's presence.

I tremble with excitement at the confident hope for a mighty cleansing move of God upon His Church. This book is indeed about hope. It's about hope for new cleansing and dynamic power for every weary, struggling Christian. It's hope for every Spirit-filled believer who longs to see revival sweep the church. It's the growing hope that Jesus is about to cleanse His Bride for a final great awakening before His glorious second coming. Yes, in spite of all that Satan is doing, we still serve the God who can shake nations. He is the God of all hope!

Writing this book has been the most humbling, yet life-changing experience of my life. By no means do I write these pages as some "lecturer of others," but as a lowly fellow learner in constant need of cleansing. In fact, God has profoundly convicted and broken my own heart during these intense days of writing. Yet, this deeper breaking has released the presence of Jesus beyond anything I have ever known. Dear reader, please believe there is hope for a far greater victory in your own life and church.

In some ways, this resource may even seem a departure from my other books on prayer, evangelism and spiritual awakening. Yet, I am convinced a serious return to holiness is actually the very heart of all powerful prayer and every nationwide spiritual awakening. Unfortunately, in today's highly programmed church, deep spiritual cleansing is either ignored entirely or quickly glossed over in a surface manner. As a result, God's people are largely unaware of the subtle, unconfessed sins that daily quench Christ's full power in their lives.

Even in most ministry initiatives, it is merely "assumed" that participants have embraced deep cleansing and prayer. In view of present society, that is an incredibly dangerous and false assumption. Indeed, many believers readily confess they're not sure how to become thoroughly cleansed and filled with God's Spirit.

Friends, if we fail to emphasize thorough cleansing, it is all too easy to end up feverishly working programs, yet without the full power of the Holy Spirit. When we thus attempt God's work in human strength, our words tend to reach men's heads but fail to penetrate their hearts. This could well be a huge reason over half of today's church members cannot be found and a disturbing number of "converts" evidence no lasting repentance. An uncleansed heart is certainly why many believers battle spiritual weariness and lack God's mountain-moving power.

According to Psalms 66:18 and Isaiah 59:1-2, lack of genuine holiness is the predominant reason God withholds His mighty presence and power. Though we have witnessed a forty-year explosion of programs and promotion, modern statistics utterly pale beside even the smallest of past Great Awakenings. Indeed, if methods and promotion alone could bring an awakening, our generation would have surely seen the biggest revival in the history of the world! Instead, we have experienced the worst moral collapse and baptism ratio decline in the life of the nation.

Yet, this book is not written from despair, but in the glorious belief God is doing something awesome! For several years, God has steadily raised a mighty prayer movement and many anointed prayer leaders. He has recently blessed with some of the most exciting soul-winning and mission tools of all time (Evangelism

Explosion, FAITH, NET, etc.). Furthermore, growing numbers of believers are beginning to hunger for deeper cleansing and greater power in prayer.

It truly seems God is setting the stage for the final element that must precede a sweeping move of revival and evangelism. And what is this key element of revival and spiritual awakening? *According to Scripture, it is nothing less than a massive return to deep repentance, fervent prayer and thorough cleansing before Holy God* (2 Chronicles 7:14). Without profound spiritual cleansing, even the most brilliant strategies are powerless to bring massive awakening to our sin-hardened nation. Even elaborate prayer strategies will have very limited power without an accompanying move of profound repentance. According to Scripture, only cleansed hearts have mighty power with God (Hosea 10:12; Psalms 66:18; James 5:16). Yet to God's praise, a glorious change is in the air!

More and more saints are embracing today's excellent strategies of prayer, missions and soul-winning. And perhaps most encouraging, growing numbers are realizing that profound cleansing and holiness are not the foreboding terms of legalism, but the essential language of a love relationship with Holy God (1 John 3:3; Hebrews 12:14). Indeed, genuine holiness brings indescribable joy and phenomenal spiritual power.

Above all, true holiness is not some abstract theological concept; holiness is a person. His name is Jesus! And if you will let Him, Jesus will fill your heart with His own glorious purity and supernatural power! Genuine holiness is not about morbid introspection, but about miraculous biblical cleansing that turns us into joyful Christians, dynamic soul winners and mountain-moving intercessors.

This book is a concise biblical tool for leading individuals and churches into the type of repentance God requires for the next Great Awakening. Above all, *Returning to Holiness* is designed as a relationship journey with God, not a rigid program. Before starting this process, it is important for readers to anticipate the awesome results that come from a such deep cleansing encounter with God. In the section below, I describe some exciting goals for every reader.

Exciting Goals for Each Reader

- To enable you to become absolutely certain of your salvation and acceptance before God
- To give you a practical, easy-to-use tool for experiencing deeper spiritual cleansing and growth on a daily basis
- To achieve practical understanding of how to confess and overcome sin in daily life
- To experience genuine victory over sin, self and Satan
- To provide a comprehensive biblical tool for discipleship, deeper holiness and biblical sanctification
- To learn how to die to self and experience the daily fullness of the Holy Spirit
- To learn how to pray biblically with mountain-moving power
- To identify and tear down your spiritual strongholds
- To provide a tool to revolutionize your daily prayer life
- To provide a tool for use in discipleship prayer groups

As you consider these goals, please note that each one is clearly something God desires for all His children. Yet surveys reveal that such are not the personal experience of most believers. It is our purpose to provide a concise, biblical tool for addressing all these vital areas. While most believers cannot wade through ten large books, many can read one that goes straight to the heart of all essential elements of personal cleansing and revival.

Returning to Holiness is further designed as a biblical strategy for overcoming churchwide sin problems. Modern churches often struggle with serious levels of apathy, disunity, immorality and worldliness. Dear believers, until we thoroughly deal with "sin in the camp," our best efforts will often seem like trying to cure cancer with a band-aid. Until we effectively address the underlying sin, God's Spirit will remain seriously quenched in our churches.

Only the direct comprehensive Word of God can bring the intense conviction and repentance that releases the cleansing flood of the Holy Spirit. A huge advantage of this tool is the ability to address many sins that would be very difficult for a pastor to confront personally. This resource also contains a powerful section for bringing many lost church members into true conviction and salvation. The following section describes the powerful goals for churchwide cleansing and renewal.

Goals and Strategies for Congregations and Pastors

- To provide pastors with a practical biblical tool to profoundly impact their own cleansing and relationship with God
- To provide a concise, biblical tool for leading the entire congregation into profound spiritual cleansing
- To provide a powerful tool for preparing the church for evangelistic crusades, revival meetings, solemn assemblies or embracing a new vision
- To provide a practical strategy for bringing unsaved church members into deep conviction and salvation
- To provide a tool for leading nonmembers and inactive members to full commitment and service
- To provide a simple tool to deepen daily cleansing and prayer among church members
- To give youth an effective tool for spiritual cleansing and strong spiritual growth
- To give members an effective tool for life-changing per-

sonal discipleship, holiness and sanctification
- To provide a flexible tool of spiritual cleansing each pastor can uniquely tailor for his own congregation
- To provide a biblical aid in preaching on a wide range of revival, discipleship and moral issues

Again, such lofty goals may sound impossible. But we must remember the awesome power of simple exposure to God's direct words from Scripture (which forms the vast majority of this book). Indeed, my words have no power whatsoever. But God's words have all power in heaven and earth!

Virtually all historic revivals and awakenings have occurred one way. *God's people were confronted with their specific sin through intense exposure to a full array of Scriptures.* Friends, let us never forget that judgement must begin at the house of God! (1 Peter 4:17) The only way this can occur is intense exposure to God's direct words at the specific points of our sin. That is precisely the unique design and purpose of this resource.

A Special Word to Pastors and Church Leaders

As a longtime pastor, I fully understand the challenges of leading a congregation into deep cleansing and revival. I realize how easy it is to schedule "revival meetings" that never become revivals. As pastors and denominational leaders, we have embraced one strategy after another and indeed seen some results. Yet inside, we long for the mighty cleansing floods we've only read about. Instinctively, we realize that such a sweeping flood is now the only hope for our sin-stricken land. But until we lead our churches to thoroughly deal with sin, such a revival can never come!

After twenty-five years of studying the Great Awakenings, I am convinced God is preparing to answer the growing prayer movement of millions of believers. I believe we are now approaching the final (and essential) phase of preparing for a glorious revival of the church. *As always, that final phase must be a much deeper return to confession, repentance and genuine holiness.*[1]

Returning to Holiness is created to provide a comprehensive cleansing tool at a low price *any* church can afford for all its youth and adult members. Indeed, the unique power of this approach is to simultaneously expose all of your active members to an intense biblical process of personal and corporate repentance. Because this resource is done completely nonprofit, it is easily affordable for large groups. In Appendix B, you will find a full description of five practical patterns for leading your church in solemn assemblies, evangelistic meetings, disciple prayer groups and a wide range of other cleansing emphases.

Pastors, one thing is certain. If our churches have any hope of true revival, it must begin with a profound new holiness in us! Despite all the training and polished organization, if we are in any part ministering in our own fleshly strength, we can never see the miraculous flood of God's power. Our churches can never go where we do not lead by personal example and experience. This resource is specifically designed to have a profound effect on the pastor's own cleansing before God.

Returning to Holiness can also be used to call associational or statewide solemn assemblies and times of cleansing. The same patterns described in Appendix B, works equally well in associationwide solemn assemblies or nights of prayer. Beyond question, God wants to mightily use association and state leaders to call thousands of churches to simultaneous repentance and prayer before Holy God. To God's praise, this is beginning to happen!

A Prayer for Every Reader

God has given a glorious invitation to all who will listen. "If my people which are called by my name, shall humble themselves, and pray, and seek my face, and turn from their wicked ways; then will I hear from heaven, and will forgive their sins, and will heal their land" (2 Chronicles 7:14). Dear reader, my fervent prayer is that you will hear and respond to God's desire to revolutionize your life. By His grace, you can meet Him through the Scriptures in this journey! Let us now respond to God's urgent call and promise in Hosea 10:12, "Sow to yourself in righteousness, reap in mercy; break up your fallow ground; for it is time to seek the Lord, until He comes and rains righteousness on you."

No words can express the urgent nature of our present need for massive revival and spiritual awakening. America is indeed poised on the very brink of catastrophic judgement. While there is reason for great hope of a coming revival, it is by no means "guaranteed." In fact, without a profound return to humility and holiness, no amount of strategy or promotion can save our land.

May God now grant us a passion for holiness — not just to "get blessed," but because we love Him. Dear saints, in the midst of all our important and needed strategies, let us not forget to wash our robes white. The harvest is wasting in the fields and the Bridegroom could be at the very door. Let us now return to God in the beauty of holiness. He is anxiously awaiting our return!

Toward the Next Great Awakening,

Gregory R. Frizzell

Preparing for
Your Journey

*Discovering
the Foundations of
Genuine Revival*

Preparing for Your
Life-Changing Journey

In spite of today's staggering moral decline, there are growing signs God is mightily touching His people. A rising number of believers and churches are seeing miraculous moves of God's Spirit. In fact, some churches are experiencing things so incredible only God can explain what is happening!

Yet, you may well ask, "If God is so mightily at work, why am I not experiencing His mighty presence and power? Why are other churches seeing such phenomenal moves of the Spirit and yet we are not?" The good news is you *can* experience God's mighty presence and power. God definitely wants to move in your life and your church!

However, there is a key requirement for experiencing God's power in your life and church. It is found in Isaiah 59:1-2: "*Behold the Lord's hand is not shortened, that it cannot save; neither His ear heavy that it cannot hear: But your iniquities have separated between you and your God, and your sins have hid His face from you, that He will not hear.*"

My friend, do you see the crucial point? Though God is willing to touch His people, unconfessed sin has blocked His mighty answers to prayer. In order to move in power, God requires deep cleansing and repentance among His people. Psalm 66:18 makes this crystal clear: "*If I regard iniquity in my heart, the Lord will not hear me.*"

If our nation is to avert much-deserved judgement, believers must immediately return to the knowledge that God is infinitely holy. He simply will not move if unconfessed sin remains in the lives of His children! For this very reason, God seems distant to many believers. Because of unconfessed sin, crucial prayers go unanswered and countless believers live in defeat and pain. If you hope to experience God's mighty power and blessing, thorough daily confession is not an option, it is absolutely essential!

The sad reality is that many believers have confession times that are far too infrequent and shallow. Because we tend to quickly rush through confession times, many sins have "built up" between us and God. Usually we are not even aware how seriously the Holy Spirit is quenched in our lives. But do not despair! Through the simple Scriptures in this book, you *can* learn to experience a level of confession and cleansing that will utterly change your life. After all, God's Word will not return void!

Thank God for the rising number of believers who desire to purify their hearts. **All across America, pastors are beginning to lead their congregations to embrace this biblical process of cleansing and repentance**. Typically it is done in a specific period ranging from one week to forty days. Some churches ask discipleship training groups to pray and work through the Scripture guide. Still others ask all active church members to pray through the resource on their own. Many churches conclude the cleansing emphasis with churchwide revival meetings or solemn assemblies. (Though that is not required.) This resource is also designed to be a preparation tool for annual revival meetings. Regardless of the format used, when God's people experience full biblical repentance, the results are phenomenal! Whether the cleansing is churchwide, small group or individual, you *will* experience an awesome release of God's presence (James 4:8).

In Isaiah 1:18, our loving Father is giving a glorious invitation to every person reading this book. *"Come now, and let us reason together, saith the Lord, though your sins be as scarlet, they shall be as white as snow; though they be red like crimson, they shall be as wool."*

In 1 John 1:9, God gives a further promise, *"If we confess our sins, he is faithful and just to forgive us our sins, and to cleanse us from all unrighteousness."* Friend, there is no reason you cannot learn to experience God's total forgiveness and cleansing on a daily basis. A victorious relationship with God is *not* out of your reach!

No matter how much you've struggled, you can experience a miraculous cleansing and filling of God's Spirit! However, this will not happen with some brief, casual prayer time. The Psalmist says you must be willing to let God *search* your heart. *"Search me, O God, and know my heart: try me, and know my thoughts: and see if there be any wicked way in me, and lead me in the way everlasting"* (Psalm 139:23-24).

Serious cleansing requires regularly getting alone with God for a thorough examination of your life. In the coming pages, you will discover a practical way *any* believer can experience deep daily cleansing. If you sincerely seek God through this simple biblical process, He will totally revolutionize your life! Yet before you begin your journey, it is crucial to grasp the foundation of your victory over sin. That foundation is none other than Jesus Christ living in you!

Christ in You – The Foundation of Victory

It is vital to understand that Jesus didn't die just to take you to heaven, but to indwell and empower you here on earth! The same God that spoke John 3:16, also spoke Romans 6:14, *"For sin shall not have dominion over you: for you are not under the law, but under grace."*

Yet, you may well be asking, "Because I struggle so much, I wonder how I could really know victory?" In Romans 6:6, Paul makes the answer beautifully clear. *"Knowing this, that our old man is crucified with Him, that the body of sin might be destroyed, that henceforth we should not serve sin."* This simple verse is the very foundation of your victory over sin.

In fact, the verses above can become your personal "declaration of independence" over the power and domination of sin. When Christ died for your sins, He not only removed the penalty of sin, but also the power. By the Holy Spirit, this same risen Christ now indwells every saved person. The Christian life is not you trying to grit your teeth and somehow live for Him, it's learning to let Him live through you! We do this through a moment by moment faith in His indwelling life and power.

Galatians 2:20 further describes the liberating truth of Christ living in us. *"I am crucified with Christ: nevertheless I live; yet not I but Christ lives in me: and the life which I now live in the flesh, I live by the faith of the Son of God, who loved me, and gave himself for me."*

Do you see it? When you receive Christ, all that He accomplished on the cross is fully alive and active in you. Because you are "in Christ," His death to sin's penalty and power is now your death to sin's penalty and power. Jesus Christ in all His victory *literally* abides within you and can live *through* you right now.

So in the coming pages, when you are convicted of sin, don't despair. Look straight to Jesus to overcome its grip. Just as you are forgiven by His sacrificial death, you are empowered by His resurrection life working in you. Let this cleansing process point you straight to Jesus and victory, not to yourself and defeat.

Yet you may well be asking, "How do I do this?" In Colossians 2:6, we find God's marvelous answer. *"As you have therefore received Christ Jesus the Lord, so walk you in him."* We walk in Christ the same way we received Him. So how did you receive Jesus? You received Him by simple faith. You simply took Jesus at His Word and trusted Him to save you. And friend, that's exactly how you walk in victory over sin and self. When you face temptation and weakness, you simply claim Christ's forgiveness and indwelling power to be your victory. You choose to turn from the sin and trust Jesus for His power to live through you. And what happens if you still feel tempted? You just keep trusting and resisting the sin. In God's time, you will see complete and total victory. Jesus Christ cannot fail!

How to Meet God Through This Book
Seven Key Points to Remember

(1) *This resource is designed as a relationship journey with God, not a program or formula.* The book is comprised largely of God's own words from Scripture. As you read and reflect on His words, God will speak directly to your heart. This book must be "prayed through" and *not* merely read. As you pray through the book, you will literally be talking to God and He will talk to you. This process is not some program you *do*, it is a relationship you *experience*. It is not a one-time activity, but a continuing journey of growth with your loving Heavenly Father.

After each Scripture, you will find questions to examine your life in light of that particular verse. It is essential that you not rush this process! As you read each Scripture, ask God to reveal what He wants to change. When He reveals a sin, immediately confess it and trust Christ for victory over that sin. Above all, do not be discouraged if you discover many areas of needed change. Our growth is a lifelong process, not a one-time event. God will definitely give you the grace to experience victory and He accepts you through the whole journey *struggles and all.*

(2) *Use a prayer notebook or journal as you work through the book.* As God reveals areas of sin, note it in your journal and be specific. (If you are concerned about confidentially, use abbreviations that are clear only to you.) Be sure to identify specific ways to overcome the sinful patterns God reveals. Remember, it is not enough merely to confess a sin, it must also be forsaken (Proverbs 28:13). For each sin you identify, find a corresponding Scripture that promises victory and strength. It is indeed vital that you *replace* a sinful pattern with a specific godly pattern. For help with this process, use a good concordance or the little book, "God's Promises for Your Every Need." By believing God's promise, you can find Christ's victory over any sin.

When you experience temptation and battle, use Scripture to resist the enemy. The Word of God is the sword of the Spirit and your weapons of warfare are mighty for the pulling down of strongholds! (2 Corinthians 10:3-5)

(3) *Specifically ask God for deep conviction of sin and clear spiritual discernment.* According to John 16:3 and 1 Corinthians 2:11, only God can bring true conviction and spiritual discernment. According to Jeremiah 17:9, we cannot even begin to know our own hearts without God's revelation. Above all, do not approach this journey as a mere mental exercise.

I also urge you to stay committed to the entire process. In

7

other words, prayerfully go through *all* the Scriptures. Today we have such a tendency to avoid serious time alone with Holy God. We surround ourselves with activity and noise and many will do almost anything to avoid a deep cleansing encounter with God. Yet, such Bible-centered encounters are essential to discipleship and holiness!

(4) *Embrace the cleansing journey as a daily relationship with God, not a one-time experience.* Daily confession and cleansing are the *essence* of walking in the Spirit! (Yet, this does not mean you are required to work through this whole booklet at one sitting.) If you are using it as a week-long preparation for a solemn assembly, you should try to move through the booklet over the period of one week. However, do not feel condemned if you don't get through the entire resource. Let God guide you at the pace He sets for you.

This scriptural resource is especially designed for use in your *daily* prayer time. In your daily quiet time, you can either pray through a couple of verses or briefly scan all the verses to see if God brings something to special awareness. When He does convict of sin, pause and focus more attention on that area.

When using this book as a part of your daily prayer time, I suggest you read and reflect on two or three Scriptures each day until you get through the entire resource. You can then start again at the beginning. In this manner, every area of your life will be thoroughly examined in continuous forty day cycles. You will be amazed how God will reveal different things each time through the resource!

I strongly suggest the use of this (or some) biblical resource to guide you in your daily cleansing and growth. This type of continual cleansing is the very essence of discipleship, growth and sanctification. Bible-centered cleansing and prayer are the primary ways we are sanctified into Christ's image. Through this process, you will experience a daily walk of supernatural holiness and power.

(5) *Approach the confession process with great assurance of God's mercy and blessing* (Isaiah 1:18). Do not be afraid of

what God might show you. Whatever sin He reveals, Christ already died for it! And God already knows about it anyway. God doesn't convict you to condemn you, but to set you free! (John 8:36)

Please do not be afraid God will ask you to do things you cannot do. He will surely give you the grace to make all the changes He requires. The mighty blessing of God will be well worth any changes He asks you to make! *Above all, do not feel overwhelmed or discouraged.* Do not feel that you must somehow become "perfect" overnight. No matter how much you have failed in the past, God will take you on a step by step journey of cleansing and renewal. This is an ongoing process and God's loving grace will cover you throughout the whole journey.

It is also important to understand that some sins may represent spiritual strongholds and could take some time to experience the full manifestation of victory. Sometimes believers think they are doing something wrong if they don't feel instantaneous victory with a single prayer or confession. Remember, this is a daily process of growth, not a one-time event. You have a kind Heavenly Father who will lovingly guide you all the way!

(6) *Be prepared for spiritual warfare* (1 Peter 5:8). According to God's Word, your spiritual enemy is very real. You need to be aware that Satan hates what you're setting out to do in this journey. He is terrified you might get clean before God and fully empowered by the Holy Spirit. He knows you will then discover awesome power in prayer and spiritual service. At all costs, Satan will fight to keep you from finishing your personal journey of revival.

Ephesians 6:11 mentions the "wiles" of the devil. That means he designs strategies to keep you from knowing and walking with God. For some, he will seek to use your busy schedule. In others, he will use discouragement and guilt. Satan will tell you, "What's the use? You're such a failure and you may as well give up." For still others, he'll try to convince you that sin's grip is too strong and you'll never be free.

But never forget, dear reader, Satan is a liar and he is defeated. At its heart, effective spiritual warfare can be boiled down to one key principle: *"Submit yourselves therefore to God, resist the devil and he will flee from you!"* (James 4:8) In other words, as you confess your sins and choose to surrender to God, you can then tell Satan "to flee" in the mighty name of Jesus Christ. Don't let Satan bluff you out of your cleansing journey with God.

(7) *Ask a trusted friend to pray for you in areas of needed change.* There is enormous power when two or more "agree together" concerning a prayer request (Matthew 18:19). If you are determined, you can find full victory for any sin God reveals in your life. Don't let pride keep you from confessing your needs and struggles to others (James 5:16). There is awesome power in united agreement and I strongly urge you to find a regular prayer partner. No matter how much you've struggled, you *will* see victory if you trust God and refuse to give up (Luke 18:1).

God's Special Invitation to You

Jeremiah 29:13 - *"And you shall seek me and find me, when you shall search for me with **all** your heart."*
James 4:8 - *"Draw nigh to God, and He **will** draw nigh to you."*

Do you hear God's awesome invitation to you and your church? God is longing to pour His holy presence and power on your life. He is longing to cleanse and set you free from the bondage of sin. He longs to sanctify and transform you into the full image of Christ (Romans 8:29; 1 Thessalonians 5:23). If you prayerfully (and honestly) work through the Scriptures in this book, God will begin that miraculous work in your life. His Word will accomplish its purpose! God will teach you how to embrace daily cleansing as a way of life and the very heart of your relationship with Him.

However, do not approach this process just to "get blessed." Do it because God is holy and He deserves your full surrender. Do it because you love Jesus and want to please Him. Do it not from a selfish motive, but with genuine desire to worship God in holiness. According to 1 John 3:3, all saved persons have a deep desire to purify themselves. Indeed, we cannot please God without a lifestyle of deep holiness. *"Follow peace with all men, and holiness, without which no man shall see the Lord"* (Hebrews 12:14).

This book focuses on bringing you into full cleansing and right relationship with God. It is also designed to *keep* you cleansed and growing in true discipleship. Yet, cleansing is only part of a dynamic love relationship with Jesus. God also intends His children to experience a vibrant, biblically-balanced prayer life!

In the Conclusion of this resource, I will show how any believer can enter into a dynamic prayer life and relationship with God. No believer should put up with a mediocre prayer life! Never forget that older children and teenagers can also experience the glorious reality of prayer! We should not sell our youth short. In many cases, they may benefit from this book even more than adults.

You will soon discover this cleansing journey is more in-depth and comprehensive than some you may have used. *It is specifically designed to bring you into a thorough search of all key areas of your life.* Incomplete confession leads to incomplete cleansing. If you allow God to do a deep daily work, you will experience life-changing discipleship!

Dear friend, God is now waiting to meet you at the point of His cleansing Word. He is ready to fully forgive and fill you with Himself. In this booklet, the Scriptures are carefully arranged to examine every category of your life. As you purposely draw near to God, be assured He will draw near to you (James 4:8). *But before you even start, pause and ask Him to speak clearly to your heart.* **Enter now into God's presence and be changed forever!**

Beginning Your Revival Journey

The Seven Categories of Cleansing

First Category
Sins of Thought

We must begin our journey with cleansing of the heart and mind. According to Scripture, sin *begins* in the heart and mind (Matthew 15:19). Until your thoughts and attitudes are under God's control, you will never know the fullness of life in Christ.

It is no accident that Satan frequently targets our minds with inappropriate, sinful thoughts. The devil knows if he can develop strongholds in our thinking, he will easily lead us into sin and separation from God's power. In Proverbs 23:7, God reveals the enormous importance of fully surrendering our minds to Christ. *"As a man thinketh in his heart, so is he."* In other words, what you think is a huge part of what you are!

Prayerfully consider the following Scriptures and honestly answer all the questions. Remember, you can only be as filled with God as you are willing to be emptied of yourself. If you are completely honest and thorough in your confession, God will completely cleanse and transform your life.

Matthew 7:22-23 - *"Many will say to me in that day, Lord, Lord, have we not prophesied in your name? And in your name cast out devils? And in your name done many wonderful works? And then will I profess to them, I never knew you; depart from me, you that work iniquity."*

John 17:3 - *"And this is life eternal, that they might know you the only true God, and Jesus Christ whom you have sent."*

Romans 8:16 - *"The Spirit itself bears witness with our spirit, that we are the children of God."*

Dear reader, as you start your cleansing journey, you must begin with the certainty of your own salvation. The first sin to overcome is doubt about your salvation. Indeed, you cannot be pleasing to God with such doubts in your heart. You can make no spiritual progress until you're absolutely certain of your relationship to Christ.

Concerning this point, the following Scriptures reveal three truths of enormous relevance: (1) On the day of judgement, Matthew 7:23 states that *many* who think they are saved will discover they do not know God; (2) According to John 17:3, true salvation consists of knowing Christ in a life-changing *personal relationship*; (3) People who are genuinely saved have a strong supernatural *assurance* of their salvation (Romans 8:16).

Tragically, in recent decades it has been all too easy for people to join churches without having a genuine salvation experience. In fact, we are now seeing many longtime church members come under conviction and find true salvation.[2] Presently, God is doing a glorious new work among unconverted church members!

If you have *any* doubt about whether you are saved, be assured that God wants to give you absolute certainty (1 John 5:13). He doesn't want you to live another day in doubt. As you answer the following questions, please be completely honest with yourself and with God. Don't just answer how you think you're "supposed" to answer. Ask God for clear discernment as you consider these crucial questions.

Questions for Reflection: Do you have nagging doubts about whether you have been saved? Do you often sense God speaking to your heart or does that idea seem foreign to you? Do you have a personal relationship with Christ or do you just know facts about Him? Can you remember a time you were deeply convicted of your lostness? Can you remember a time when you truly turned from sin and personally surrendered your life to Jesus? When you made your profession of faith, did you experience a noticeable change in your life? Do you have absolute peace that you are forgiven and going to heaven? Do you have a significant desire for Bible reading and prayer? Do you have a longing to be in church and with God's people? Are you known as a person of kindness and love?

If you had to honestly answer *no* to many of the above questions, it is essential that you stop now and settle your relationship with Christ. The good news is you can settle it! God is willing and able to give you the assurance you so desperately need. If you have any doubt whatsoever about your salvation, I urge you to turn to page 87 and prayerfully work through Appendix A (*How to be Certain of Your Salvation*) before going one step further! Through His clear promises, God wants to lead every reader to perfect assurance and peace.

If you answered *yes* to the questions, then immediately proceed with your cleansing journey. You can confidently rejoice that Jesus' blood cleanses you from all unrighteousness. Rejoice that your eternal security is in Jesus' perfect righteousness and *not* your imperfect performance. Let's continue your journey by examining other key areas of thought.

---

2 Corinthians 10:5 - *"Casting down imaginations and every high thing that exalteth itself against the knowledge of God, and bringing into captivity **every thought** to the obedience of Christ."*

Questions for Reflection: Carefully and honestly reflect on the type of thoughts that occupy your mind. Is your mind filled with thoughts of Christ or consumed with earthly issues? Do you think far more about work or recreation than spiritual growth and serving Christ? Are you often filled with unclean thoughts? Are you plagued with fearful or angry thoughts? Write down any sinful thought pattern God brings to your attention. For each one, ask God's forgiveness and trust Him to renew your mind (Romans 12:2). Resolve to take every thought captive to the Lordship of Christ. What specific thoughts should replace the ones that are worldly?

Matthew 5:28 - *"But I say unto you, That whosoever looks on a woman to lust after her hath committed adultery with her already in his heart."*

Questions for Reflection: Do lustful, unclean thoughts frequently occupy your mind? Do you watch programs or movies that stimulate improper thoughts and feelings? Are you conscious of unclean thoughts or motives? Do you often have thoughts you would be ashamed for others to know? Do you have wandering eyes?

If you sense God's conviction, be *specific* in your confession. Decide how you are going to change your thoughts to remove the patterns of sin. Be specific about the thoughts you need to change. It is vital that you *replace* unclean thoughts with other thoughts that focus on Christ. Memorizing key Scriptures will provide a powerful tool for removing inappropriate thoughts. Every time an unclean thought arises, you can replace it with Scripture and a prayerful focus on God. If you follow this process, you will soon have a brand new mind! (Romans 12:2)

Colossians 3:1-3 - *"If you then be risen with Christ, seek those things which are above, where Christ sitteth on the right hand of God. Set your **affection** on things above, not on things on the earth."*

According to Matthew 22:37, Jesus and His work should occupy first place in our daily thoughts and affections. Jesus said we are to love Him with "all our heart, soul, mind and strength." If Christ is truly your passion, your mind will be filled with thoughts of serving Him.

Questions for Reflection: Do your affections and priorities often revolve around people and things more than Jesus? Are you more passionate about earthly things rather than spiritual things? Do you honestly get more excited about work, sports or recreation than about God's kingdom? To what or to whom do you devote the majority of your thoughts and energies? Is Christ central in all your priorities, or does He occupy only a small corner of your thoughts and plans? If many of your thoughts are undisciplined and earth-centered, immediately confess this to God and ask Him to transform your mind. By God's grace, you can change your affections and thoughts! Write down specific ways you need to set your affections and thoughts on Jesus.

Psalm 1:2 - *"But his delight is in the law of the Lord; and in his law doth he meditate day and night."*

Psalm 119:15-16 - *"I will meditate in thy precepts, and have respect unto thy ways. I will delight myself in thy statutes: I will not forget thy word."*

Based on these Scriptures, it is God's will for every believer to saturate his mind with key Bible verses. Yet, filling your mind with Scripture does not happen by accident. You must make a daily choice to hide God's Word in your heart.

Questions for Reflection: Is it your habit to seriously read and study God's Word daily? Do you meditate on key verses or does God's Word have little place in your thoughts? Have you failed to write down key verses that speak to special needs in your life? Filling your mind with Scripture requires a consistent choice. You cannot love God and yet not love His Word. In a very real sense, to neglect God's Word is to neglect God. Confess the sin of failing to fill your mind with Scripture. (Consider using the booklet, **God's Promises for Every Need**) If you get Scripture into your daily thoughts, God will revolutionize your life! (John 15:7) Make a personal commitment to embrace a Scripture memorization plan.

James 4:3 - *"You ask, and receive not, because you ask amiss, that you may consume it upon your lusts."*

Improper motive is a sin frequently overlooked. Very likely, it is the unrecognized cause of many unanswered prayers. Indeed, it is all too common for people to treat God like a mail-order catalog. We constantly give Him our list of wants, but have little thought of what we can give to Him. We always want Him to *do* things for us, but are not nearly as concerned with what we can do *for* Him. Many people pray and worship with very selfish motives. We almost treat God like a "magic genie" to manipulate for what we want.

Questions for Reflection: Are you guilty of seeking God more for what He can do for you than out of genuine love for Him? Do you sense your thoughts are mixed with selfish desires rather than seeking God's glory? Are you aware of the desire to be noted and praised by people rather than mainly seeking God's pleasure? Are you unwilling to pray for God's will, when it does not fit your plan? Does your love and worship decrease when things don't go your way? When you get disappointed, do you "cool off" toward God and church? If so, this reveals a significant level of impure motive.

If you are convicted of selfish, impure or shallow motives, immediately confess these sins. Ask God to grant you a deep purity of purpose for His kingdom. Ask Him to give you "unconditional" love and service to Himself. If you trust Christ, the Holy Spirit will fill your heart with a pure, unconditional love of God (Romans 5:5).

Matthew 15:8-9a - *"This people draw nigh to me with their mouth, and honor me with their lips: but their heart is far from me. But in vain they do worship me."*

Amos 5:21-24 - *"I hate, I despise your feast days, and I will not savor your solemn assemblies. Though you offer me burnt offerings and your meat offerings, I will not accept them."*

The above passages reveal God's extreme displeasure with insincere worship and empty ritual. The very essence of worship is to *bow* before God in genuine reverence and surrender. Yet, even many believers have forgotten the awesome holiness and majesty of our Creator. To some, it's as if God exists mostly to fulfill all our desires and needs. We seriously compromise with sin and yet still expect God to honor our prayers and receive our worship. It seems many have forgotten that willful, habitual sin is equal to *"trampling underfoot the precious blood of Jesus"* (Hebrews 10:29).

It is further disturbing to see how thoughtlessly many receive the Lord's Supper. The Lord's Supper is a moment of supreme holiness and personal examination. In 1 Corinthians 11:28-30,

Paul even states that sickness and death can result from irreverence for Christ's sacrifice. Yet many approach this holy moment with absolutely no thought of confession or repentance. The fact that God could bring catastrophic judgement seems never to cross the minds of most modern saints.

Still others treat the Sabbath as just another day to work, shop or recreate. Even some who call themselves serious Christians completely forget to keep the day holy unto the Lord.[3] We forget that deep reverence for the Lord's day is one of God's ten basic commandments. Genuine reverence for God has been largely abandoned by many modern believers. Most are oblivious to just how far we have moved from a biblical reverence for God.

Questions for Reflection: In coming to worship, is your primary purpose to *bow* before God in utter repentance and obedience? Is your mind filled with holy fear and reverence for God? Do you really love and reverence God or mostly just seek His benefits? Do you set aside all of Sunday for God or merely tip your hat for an hour before doing your own thing? Have you taken the Lord's Supper without deep examination and personal repentance? Do you frequently sing the worship hymns without deeply reflecting on the words? Do you listen to sermons with little thought of immediate obedience to God's instructions? Insincere, ritualistic worship is one of the most serious sins a believer can commit! Do you need to confess a shallow reverence and worship of God? Immediately confess this most serious of sins. Trust God to grant you the spirit of genuine reverence and worship.

Hebrews 12:14 - *"Pursue peace with all men, and **holiness**, without which no man shall see the Lord."*

1 John 3:3 - *"And every man that hath this hope in him **purifies** himself, even as he is pure."*

The intense pursuit of holiness is to be the predominant priority of every Christian. Actually the pursuit of holiness is a spiritual *mindset*. The Greek word for "pursuit" means an intense or passionate effort. If someone is Spirit-filled, there will be a burning thirst to experience Christ's holiness in every corner of his being. Serious daily Bible reading and prayer are the primary means by which we pursue such purity and growth. Friend, if you are not focused on continually deepening your prayer life and Bible study, then you are *not* pursuing holiness. Seeking God's holiness is a daily action, not a theological theory.

Questions for Reflection: Is your mind filled with thoughts of how to experience greater holiness? Do you often say, "I wish I was more like Jesus" and then do little to pursue spiritual cleansing? Do you consistently make time to allow God to search every area of your life? God's Word is absolutely central to this process. Do you regularly read comprehensive lists of Scriptures designed to thoroughly examine your heart? If not, then you are not seriously pursuing holiness. In Matthew 6:33, Jesus said we are to, "*Seek first the kingdom of God and His righteousness.*" Is holiness your top pursuit? If not, ask God to grant you a heart that hungers for a holiness that is genuine. That's one prayer God will answer every time!

Personal Reflection on
Sins of Thought

1. Go back and review the specific Scriptures through which God brought special conviction. What thoughts did God tell you to change? Which ones do you need to address first? Be specific and list them below.

2. How do these sins affect your relationship with God and others?

3. Ask God to give you Scripture promises to help you overcome each sin. List them below.

4. In what specific ways are you prepared to change your thoughts? What thoughts will replace those that are improper? List them below.

Second Category
Sins of Attitude

As God examines our lives, He not only views our outward actions, He especially watches the attitude behind them. Indeed, many times "how" someone says something carries almost as much weight as what they actually say. God is deeply focused on the attitude of our hearts. In a very real sense, everyone has an attitude (or spirit) about them. Ask God to clearly open your eyes to the heart attitudes within.

Revelation 3:15-16 - *"I know thy works, that you are neither cold nor hot: I would thou wert cold or hot. So then because thou art lukewarm, and neither cold nor hot, I will spue thee out of my mouth."*

It is clear that God desires a fervent and passionate love from His children. In fact, the attitude of lukewarmness literally *nauseates* God. We must understand that the root of all sin is a lack of fervent love for Christ. The very root of sin is the love and worship of self over God.

Questions for Reflection: Can you truly categorize your love and service to God as passionate? Is God and His service the burning priority in your life? On a scale of 1-10, how would you rate your zeal for Christ? Are you on fire for prayer? Are you deeply excited about Bible study, witnessing and serving God? Was there a time you loved and served God more fervently than now? If you sense any lukewarmness, honestly confess this sin to God. Only the Holy Spirit can grant you pure burning love for Jesus. Pray in faith for God to give you a heart that burns with passion for Him. If you are sincere, He will forgive and give you a brand new heart! (Ezekiel 36:26)

---

1 Peter 5:5 - *"God resists the proud, but gives grace to the humble."*

Psalm 51:17 - *"A broken and contrite heart, O God, you will not despise."*

Pride is a subtle sin so easily overlooked. Perhaps the worse form of pride is the attitude of spiritual complacency that sees little need for cleansing and growth in one's own life. True revival always begins with deep humility and brokenness over sin (2 Chronicles 7:14).

Questions for Reflection: Do you think yourself quite spiritual? Do you often criticize and judge others? Are you frequently trying to set others straight? Do you spend daily time allowing God to deeply search your life or do you feel you need little cleansing? Are you truly broken and contrite over your shortcomings or do you think, "Oh well, no one is perfect"?

Are you desperately hungry to see a mighty move of God or are you somewhat complacent? Do you come across as having a "holier than thou attitude?" If you feel that you have nearly "arrived" and need little growth, you are guilty of the worst form of spiritual pride. God hates self-righteousness and spiritual complacency. Immediately confess and forsake the sin of pride. Believe Christ for a spirit of genuine humility and contriteness of heart.

Philippians 2:3-4 - *"Let nothing be done through strife or vainglory: but in lowliness of mind let each esteem others better than themselves. Look not every man on his own things, but every man also on the things of others."*

Questions for Reflection: Do you tend to draw attention to yourself? Do you often promote yourself and put others down? Are you highly competitive and desire to win and be number one at all costs? Do you seek to be the center of attention? Do you usually think mostly in terms of your own needs and desires? Is your attitude such that you feel you are better and smarter than others? Do you have an inordinate need to be noticed and praised by people? Do you tend to surround yourself with "status symbols" that flaunt wealth or appearance?

God hates all forms of arrogance and self-exaltation (Proverbs 8:13, 1 Peter 5:5). If you sense God's conviction, immediately confess and forsake this sin. Be specific and write down changes God wants you to embrace.

James 2:1,4 - *"My brethren, have not the faith of our Lord Jesus Christ, the Lord of glory, with respect of persons...Are you not then partial in yourselves, and are become judges of evil thoughts?"*

In the above Scripture, we note the extreme importance of rejecting sins of prejudice and partiality. Because each person has great value to God, believers should never harbor hostility or prejudice toward those of different race, physical appearance or economic standing. It is profoundly wrong to pre-judge and devalue other persons. Tragically, prejudice comes in many subtle forms and is all too common among believers. Some believers arrogantly believe they can even judge the inner motives of others. In many cases, such sins of prejudice go wholly unrecognized and unconfessed.

Questions for Reflection: Do you associate only with those very similar to yourself? Do you tend to look down on people who are not as financially affluent? Conversely, do you resent those who have more monetarily? Do you closely associate only with your own race or culture? Are you suspicious of those from a differenct race, culture or background? Do you think you are too good to befriend someone who is physically unattractive? Do you tend to resent people more physically attractive or gifted than yourself? Have you sought to reach out to other culture groups or have you settled into a social "comfort zone"?

Has your church placed too high a premium on reaching certain classes of people? Though we can disguise it with rationalizations, we must reject any tendency to avoid certain segments of society. Have you placed an inordinate emphasis on reaching the more affluent?

For the sake of balance, let me state that it's understandable for people to have closer associations with those similar to themselves. Such natural cultural affinities do not necessarily indicate prejudice. However, if you harbor any hostilities or *willful* avoidance of others, you are indeed guilty of prejudice and partiality. If you seldom reach out to other groups, you stand in serious need of confession and repentance.

Hebrews 11:6 - *"But without faith it is impossible to please him: for he that cometh to God must believe that he is, and that he is a rewarder of them that diligently seek him."*

Unbelief is one of the most deadly sins a believer can commit. It was unbelief that caused the children of Israel to die in the wilderness. Unbelief immediately short-circuits God's power in the believer's life. Because of unbelief, many believers live in weakness and defeat. Through lack of faith, crucial prayers go unanswered (Matthew 13:58).

Questions for Reflection: Are you often filled with more doubt than faith? Do you tend to worry and fret rather than trust God? Are you fully resting in God's promises or are you frequently anxious? Have you *excused* the sin of unbelief by claiming to be a "born worrier"? Do you excuse your doubt by saying, "I have good reason to worry"? Have you let disappointments weaken your faith and prayer life? A pattern of worry is not just a weakness, it is a willful sin against God. God promises perfect peace to those who choose to trust rather than fear (Isaiah 26:3). Do you need to confess the sin of unbelief and worry? (You may also need to talk to a godly counselor or doctor about the roots of your anxiety.) No matter how long you've doubted, God can give you true faith and a supernatural peace. Don't settle for anything less!

Ephesians 4:2 - *"With all lowliness and **kindness**, with longsuffering, forbearing one another in love."*

The primary mark of a Spirit-filled believer is a kind, loving spirit. The primary mark of a carnal believer is a critical, angry attitude. A sure sign of carnality is a loud, pushy attitude which demands its own way.

Questions for Reflection: Do you have a kind, gentle spirit or are you argumentative and contentious? Are you often critical and harsh with people? Are you often insensitive to the feelings and needs of others? Do you tend to look for reasons to pick people apart? Are you quick to get angry and speak your mind? A gentle and quiet spirit is valued of great price to God (1 Peter 3:4). Do others characterize you as having a gentle and quiet spirit? Are you quick to point out the weaknesses of others? Do you make excuses by saying, "I can't help it, that's just my personality?" Be honest in your evaluation of your heart attitude. Ask for God's forgiveness and cleansing. Be specific about ways to change your attitude. (Especially with family.)

---

1 Corinthians 13:4(a), 7 - *"Love suffers long and is kind, it bears all things, believes all things, hopes all things, endures all things."*

Matthew 5:44 - *"But I say to you, Love your enemies, bless them that curse you, do good to them that hate you, and pray for them which spitefully use you, and persecute you."*

A forgiving attitude is a primary mark of someone right with God. However, it is all too common for people to be highly religious, yet possess a judgmental, unloving spirit. Pharisees come in many shapes and varieties. Through lack of love and unforgiveness, family members often build relationship barriers in their homes. Though we may "say" we forgive, we really don't.

Questions for Reflection: Do you respond with forgiveness and love when someone hurts you? Do you make a point of actively doing good to those who have done you evil? Are you carrying an internal catalogue of grievances against friends or family members? Do you brood on the ways a spouse or child has disappointed you? Do you withhold your kindness because they don't "deserve" it? Do you give loved ones the "silent treatment"? Have you determined to love family and friends with Christ's unconditional love?

My friend, your places of disappointment are your greatest opportunity to let Jesus live through you. In just such times, you will experience your greatest growth or worst failure. Trust Jesus to fill your heart with His pure, unconditional love for others.

---

1 Timothy 6:6 - *"But godliness with contentment is great gain....And having food and raiment let us be therewith content."*

1 John 2:15-17 - *"Love not the world, neither the things that are in the world. If any man love the world, the love of the Father is not in him. For all that is in the world, the lust of the flesh, and the lust of the eyes, and the pride of life, is not of the Father, but is of the world."*

Materialism and worldliness are among the most pervasive (yet unacknowledged) sins of modern Christians. Quite often, believers are blind to the materialism that subtly saturates our very souls. Rather than adhering to God's standard of moderation, high debt has become the norm. Many believers truly covet the symbols of worldly status and wealth. Indeed, our very affluence has become a huge spiritual hindrance. We have indeed moved far from Paul's simple command, *"Be content with such things as you have"* (Hebrews 13:5).

Questions for Reflection: Do you barely tithe and yet pay enormous interest to creditors? In purchases, have you been motivated more by greed than seeking God's direction? Does your financial history reflect biblical principles of low debt and modest living? Has your debt caused you to miss payments and thus damage your witness? Do you lust for things? Would you be willing to live with less in order to embrace more God-centered patterns for your money? Financial pressures strain many marriages.[4] Is high debt straining yours?

Can you truly say "Jesus Christ is in control of my desires and finances"? Have you fervently prayed about financial decisions or simply gone with the materialism of the world? Today there are excellent books and resources to help you reduce debt and break the bondage to covetousness. Please do not ignore God's conviction in this crucial area of your life! Be specific about the changes God wants you to embrace. Take a moment and decide on your first steps of financial repentance.

Personal Reflection on
Sins of Attitude

1. Go back and review the specific Scriptures through which God brought special conviction. What attitudes did God tell you to change? Which ones do you need to especially address first? Be specific and list them below.

2. How do these sins affect your relationship with God and others?

3. Ask God to give you Scripture promises to help you overcome each sin. List them below.

4. In what specific ways are you prepared to change your attitude? What attitudes will replace those that are improper?

Third Category
Sins of Speech

God places enormous importance on our speech. In Matthew 12:36, Jesus makes a sobering statement. *"But I say unto you, That every idle word that men shall speak, they shall give account of in the day of judgment."* Today's society has experienced an unprecedented explosion of vile and wicked speech.[5] Often without even knowing it, many believers have become involved in significant sins of speech. Ask God for discernment as you prayerfully examine your words.

Ephesians 4:29 - *"Let no corrupt word proceed out of your mouth."*

Ephesians 5:4 - *"Neither filthiness, nor foolish talking, not jesting, which are not convenient; but rather giving of thanks."*

Questions for Reflection: Do you ever speak slang words that are crude and inappropriate? Do you use God's name in any way other than worship, honor and praise? Have you engaged in off-color jokes or conversation? Has the filthiness of our society crept into your speech? Do you use any slang to add emphasis to what you're saying? In Matthew 5:37, Jesus clearly stated the use of slang is wrong. Honestly examine your speech and ask God for His forgiveness. Be specific in your confession of improper speech. Fully surrender your speech to the Lordship of Jesus Christ.

Colossians 3:9 - *"Lie not one to another, seeing that you have put off the old man with his deeds."*

Questions for Reflection: Do you ever lie? Do you exaggerate to make yourself look better? Are you guilty of any form of cheating? Do you mislead people or institutions? Are you careful to follow through with promises, vows and commitments you make to God and others? Is your word your bond or are you somewhat unreliable? Do you frequently fall short in things you said you would do? If so, this reveals an integrity problem. God hates lying and inconsistency. Fully confess and renounce any patterns of untruthfulness or unreliability.

---

1 Corinthians 10:10 - *"Let us not murmur and complain as some of them also murmured and were destroyed of the destroyer."*

1 Thessalonians 5:18 - *"In every thing give thanks: for this is the will of God in Christ Jesus concerning you."*

The children of Israel continually complained about God's provision. As a result, they perished in the wilderness. As Christians, we are definitely commanded to rejoice and give thanks in all things (1 Thessalonians 5:18). A lifestyle of continual praise is *essential* to pleasing God.

It is impossible to be a "complainer" and walk in the power of God's Spirit.

Questions for Reflection: Do you often gripe and complain about situations in your life? Do you fail to give thanks in all things and at all times? Are you filled with an attitude of gratefulness and praise or grumbling and complaining? Do you make excuses for your grumbling by saying, "I have good reason to complain?" Are you always looking on the dark sides of things? Do you trust God for supernatural joy or do you give in to murmuring and complaining?

Such an attitude is a major sin and blocks God's full blessing on your life. Friend, if you are willing to change, God will give you a miraculous joy! (You may also need to visit a godly counselor or doctor to insure that clinical depression is not a factor.) If you will praise Him, God promises to give supernatural joy in spite of difficult circumstances. Be specific about ways you need to rejoice and give thanks.

Ephesians 4:31 - *"Let all bitterness, and wrath, and anger and clamor, and evil speaking, be put away from you, with all malice."*

A tragic modern trend is the rising number of church fights and congregational splits.[6] What is the cause of this spiritual scourge? The most obvious cause is that the world's patterns have infiltrated the church. In today's society, people are so ready to fight, break vows or even sue at the drop of a hat. God intends for His church to be different! We are to be a place of healing and transformation, not a place to continue the bickering. Thank God, more and more believers are beginning to confess their sins and find a glorious victory. Beyond question, you can too! Please honestly answer the following questions.

Questions for Reflection: Are you guilty of critical, angry speech? Do you argue and fight with others? Do you tend to be irritable and cranky? Are you quick to raise your voice? Does your speech reflect an underlying anger and impatience with those around you? Do you speak unkindly to those in your family? Are you guilty of any form of gossip or slander of others? Do you speak evil of people behind their back? Immediately confess and forsake these serious sins of speech.

---

1 Corinthians 1:10 - *"Now I beseech you, brethren, by the name of our Lord Jesus Christ, that you all speak the same thing, and that there be no divisions among you; but that you be perfectly joined together in the same mind and in the same judgment."*

Today one of Satan's most effective tools is getting believers to divide and fight. Often Christians argue over things that are not even important. A sure sign of sin and immaturity is a divisive, contentious spirit. A primary commandment of believers is to "love one another"! According to Scripture, we are to put the desires and needs of others ahead of our own. It is impossible to be Spirit-filled and yet have an argumentative, contentious spirit. If believers would simply walk in the principle of love, there might not be church divisions and fighting.

Nothing dishonors Christ or pleases Satan more than bickering among God's people. Tragically, in church fights there are certain individuals who always seem to be at the root of it. Though they are the small minority, these individuals often quench the Holy Spirit for an entire church. They are so quick to see the speck in a brother's eye, but virtually blind to the board in their own (Luke 6:41-42). Unfortunately, they are usually so spiritually blinded and immature, that they convince themselves they are "fighting" for a good cause.

Questions for Reflection: Are you known as a peacemaker who strengthens church unity or, are you often part of some contentious argument? Do you act like a "self-appointed" critic and judge to set everyone else straight? Are you quick to talk about the shortcomings of others? Do you increase the faith of your church by a positive attitude or, do you tear it down by focusing on its imperfections? Are you quick to divide up and "take sides"? Do you tend to be a part of church cliques? Are you known as a complainer and one who is easily upset? Have you been critical and condemning of those with different tastes in music and worship style?

Such subtle sins of attitude and speech are often more damaging to a church than obvious outward sins. In truth, a negative church member can often do more damage than an alcoholic! Does God convict you of any tendency to be contentious, divisive or negative? *Do not make excuses or justify your behavior.* If you are honest in your confession and repentance, God will totally transform your heart. He will give you wisdom to deal with honest differences of opinion without becoming angry and divisive. God will also lead you to ask forgiveness from those you have offended (Matthew 5:23-24).

---

1 Timothy 5:17 - *"Let the elders that rule well be counted worthy of double honor, especially they who labor in the word and doctrine."*

This generation has witnessed a shocking increase of preachers and lay-leaders being fired or mistreated for small, (often exaggerated) reasons.[7] *Certainly when a leader sins, he or she must be dealt with.* Yet today, many churches have forgotten the biblical principle of respect and honor for those who lead the church. In many churches, the Holy Spirit is quenched because the congregation has sinned against a pastor or church leader.

When churches experience revival, they often must seek forgiveness from pastors or leaders they may have mistreated. Many churches may also need to ask forgiveness from a former pastor or lay-leader. (In other cases, pastors must ask the forgiveness of churches they have wronged.)

A glorious and growing trend is the number of churches that are getting right with other congregations that formed as "a split" from their own. This does not mean churches have to reunite, but it does mean they *must* fully forgive past offenses. Until you get right with those you fought in the past, there will not be full blessing on your church or your life!

Questions for Reflection: Have you been critical or slanderous of Christians leaders? Do you fail to respect and honor those called to lead the church? Do you undermine their authority? Do you tend to "pick them apart" rather than give consistent encouragement and prayer support? Are there leaders or other believers with whom you've parted on angry terms? Do you tend to slander or mock other denominational groups, ministries or leaders who may not agree with you on every point? God *will not* fill your life until such sins are fully confessed and forsaken!

Personal Reflection on
Sins of Speech

1. Go back and review the specific Scriptures through which God brought conviction. What patterns of speech do you need to change? Be specific and list them below.

2. How do these sins affect your relationship with God and others? Be specific.

3. What Scripture promises will you claim to help you overcome each sin? List some below.

4. In what specific ways are you prepared to change your speech? What speech patterns will replace the sinful patterns?

Fourth Category
Sins of Relationships

Perhaps the most common place we lose God's fullness is in our relationships. Relationship sins generally fall in five major areas. In each area, you must be willing to take specific actions of repentance. But by God's mighty grace, you can!

Can you think of people you may have hurt or offended in some manner?

In Matthew 5:23-24, Jesus was emphatic about the importance of getting right with those you have offended. *"Therefore, if you bring your gift to the altar, and there remember that your brother has something against you, leave your gift before the altar, and go your way. **First** be reconciled to your brother, and **then** come and offer your gift."*

In other words, Christ was saying, "Don't approach God until you first get right with those you have offended!" Friend, I am not suggesting this is easy, but Christ clearly says it is absolutely *necessary*. Many Christians lack power because they have ignored this foundational command.

Take the next several moments to consider those you may have offended. *When God reveals people you have hurt or slighted, resolve to go to them and ask their forgiveness.* Yet, do not go and try to defend yourself or get the battle started again. Just go in simple humility and love. Furthermore, do not think you have failed if they refuse to forgive you. Your responsibility is to do your part in a humble and loving manner. How they respond is their responsibility.

Tremendous miracles occur in families when someone is humbly willing to ask forgiveness for a wrong. Powerful churchwide revivals have often hinged on one or two church members getting truly right with one another. *We must understand that so-called "little" rifts between Christians can easily quench God's*

Spirit for the whole church! Friend, the Holy Spirit is very sensitive and you must take your relationships seriously.

Are you bitter or holding grudges against people who have offended you?

In Matthew 6:14-15, Jesus made a statement of enormous importance. *"For if you forgive men their trespasses, your heavenly Father will also forgive you. But if you do not forgive men their trespasses, neither will your Father forgive your trespasses."*
Many a prayer gets no higher than the ceiling because you are holding inner resentment and bitterness against another person. In fact, Jesus says we must forgive people "from the heart." Matthew 18:35, *"So my heavenly Father also will do to you, if each of you from his heart, does not forgive his brother his trespasses."* It is common for people to "say" they have forgiven someone when in their heart, they really haven't.
Many people hold secret bitterness against friends or family members. In other cases, it may be toward strangers who have wronged you. Especially today, believers need to be aware that we can develop bitterness toward godless politicians, social activists, and entertainers who attack our values. No doubt, we must always stand strong for truth, but we must never harbor hatred against those who attack us. We must never cease to hate sin, but we must always love the sinner. Ask God to search your heart and reveal any patterns of bitterness or unforgiveness.
It is also possible to hold secret bitterness against God. Some people privately resent the fact that God allowed some personal tragedy or didn't answer an urgent prayer. Others harbor bitterness because God blesses others in ways He has not blessed them. Far too many Christians have cooled off in their service and worship because they are hurt or disappointed.

Questions for Reflection: Is there anyone or any situation about which you harbor the slightest bitterness or resentment? Have you secretly resented God for allowing some painful situation in your life? Have you "cooled off" toward God because He disappointed you in some manner? Be honest with yourself and fully confess these sins. Make a definite decision to harbor no bitterness against anyone. And remember, forgiveness is a *choice*, not a *feeling*. Yet if you choose to forgive, God will change your feelings.

Are you involved in any improper relationships?

An improper relationship could be anything from adultery and fornication to simply being inappropriately close to someone. For example, a young person may be emotionally involved with someone too old or vice versa. A husband may be too emotionally close to a female friend or work mate. A wife may be too emotionally involved with a male friend or work mate. Husbands and wives may be sharing things with others that should only be shared with their mate. Spouses may spend too much time with friends to the neglect of their marriage partner. Parents can be too involved in the lives of their married children or married children too dependent on parents.

You may be involved with someone and while you say "we're just friends," you know it has become more than friendship. Don't try to rationalize or defend a relationship you know is improper. It inevitably opens the door to Satan and leads you into ever-deepening bondage.

Improper relationships involve many things **besides** *physical immorality*. Because it's so easy to rationalize, this sin has become prevalent among Christians. It is the soil from which adultery and fornication so often grow. Ask God to reveal any relationships that are improper or out of balance. It is vital that you stop it now before it gets worse. Be honest with God and with yourself. And, do not despair, God will give you the strength to change!

Do you neglect regular fellowship and meaningful service through your church?

According to Hebrews 10:25, it is a major sin to neglect regular fellowship and worship with the body of Christ. *"Not forsaking the assembling of ourselves together, as is the manner of some, but exhorting one another, and so much the more, as you see the day approaching."*

God strongly emphasizes the importance of staying closely connected to a local body of believers. According to 1 Corinthians 12-14, all believers are to stay in genuine fellowship and close relationship with a local congregation.

God does not intend for anyone to be a "lone ranger" or an "isolationist"! In our day of selfish individualism, many people like to join a large church so they can get lost in the crowd.[8] They come and receive blessings, but then go home without any real fellowship or closeness with other believers. (And that's exactly the way they want it!) Such a pattern is totally unbiblical and inherently selfish.

Still others seek a church that will "bless them" without asking how they can serve or give in return. Many people selfishly shop for a church like they shop for a health club. They want one with the most benefits and least cost! Churches in growing areas usually have people running out their ears, while churches in tough areas (where ministry is so needed) often starve for Christian workers.

Today it seems many want to sit and be served, but few want to get up and serve. In seeking a church, our primary prayer should not be "What can this church do for me," but rather "what can I do for this church?" *It is a major sin not to be involved in consistent giving and service through a local body of believers.* Obviously, this principle does not apply to the homebound or seriously ill. Also there are exceptions in the case of those called to itinerant ministries. (Yet, even they need a definite home church!)

Another common form of this sin is the tendency to *drift* from church to church. Such people often become permanent *visitors*. By doing this, these believers never form deep biblical fellowship with other Christians. They also avoid personal responsibility and spiritual service for the good of Christ's Church. As a result, they can never grow up spiritually or be truly right with

God. Unfortunately, Satan often deceives such people into believing they are somehow fulfilling their responsibility to Christ's body. Ask God to search your life and reveal ways you are neglecting consistent fellowship and substantial service in the local body of Christ.

Questions for Reflection: Are you a spectator rather than a participant in God's work? Do you consistently receive, but seldom give? Have you become a permanent visitor who never seems to plug in and serve God? Friend, if you want to be right with God, you *must* decide to embrace a church and go to work! Resolve now to immediately obey God in full commitment to a local body of believers.

Are your family relationships consistent with God's Word?

Improper family and church relationships are common places we lose the filling and power of God's Spirit. *"No one who is wrong with others can be truly right with God."* The following Scripture reveal God's plumb line for husbands, wives and children.

God's special words to husbands and fathers - Ephesians 5:23 - *"For the husband is the head of the wife, even as Christ is the head of the church."*

From this verse we see that God calls the husband to be the spiritual head of the home. He is responsible to give spiritual guidance and nurture. Every husband and father has a very special responsibility to God and to his family.

Ephesians 5:25 - *"Husbands, love your wives, even as Christ also loved the church and gave himself for it."*

The husband is commanded to love his wife with a powerful, sacrificial love. He is to literally sacrifice himself to meet the needs of his wife. The husband is to "give himself" to meet the physical, emotional and spiritual needs of his wife. In every way, he is to place the needs and welfare of his wife ahead of his own.

1 Peter 3:7 - *"Likewise, you husbands, dwell with them according to knowledge, giving honor unto the weaker vessel."*

The husband is commanded to be very caring and sensitive to his wife's needs. A husband's uncaring, insensitive attitude toward his wife will inevitably hinder his ability to pray (1 Peter 3:7). A godly husband will literally study the unique needs and desires of his wife. This includes physical, emotional, mental, financial and spiritual needs.

Ephesians 6:4 - *"And you fathers, provoke not your children to wrath: but bring them up in the nurture and admonition of the Lord."*

The father is commanded to relate to his children in loving spiritual guidance, not in anger or wrath. Discipline must done with consistency and love. The father's great priority is the spiritual nurture and training of his family. It is certainly important, but financial provision is by *no means* the father's primary responsibility.

Questions for Reflection: Husband, have you taken responsibility to lead your family in devotions and prayer? Do you set a loving atmosphere of spiritual nurture and training? Do you put your wife's needs and desires ahead of your own? Do you study to understand and meet the unique emotional needs of your wife? Have you made use of today's excellent books and videos on marriage? Are you providing wise financial guidance and stewardship for the security of your family? Are you guiding your children in spiritual growth and training? Do you discipline your children with consistency and love? Do you consistently talk to your children about spiritual values? (A brief daily devotion alone can never replace the value of consistent conversation with your children about everyday life issues.)

Let no husband despair! If you honestly confess your failures, God will give you the powerful grace to change. Today, there are many good books and resources to help you. Don't be overwhelmed even though you may feel inept. God will bless even small steps toward fulfilling your spiritual responsibility. Husband, you can see a miracle in your family!

God's special words to wives - Ephesians 5:24,33 - *"Therefore as the church is subject to Christ, so let the wives be to their own husbands in everything...and the wife see that she reverence her husband."*

The submission of the wife does not mean the husband can be a harsh master or boss over her. They are equal partners in the grace of Christ. Rather, her submission is the loving and willing submission seen with Christ and His Church. Thus, a godly wife exhibits a beautiful spirit of humility, love and honor toward her husband. She is to have a "gentle and quiet" spirit.

1 Peter 3:3 - *"Whose adorning let it not be that outward adorning of plaiting the hair, and of wearing of gold, or of putting on of apparel, but let it be the hidden man of the heart, in that which is not corruptible, even the ornament of a meek and quiet spirit, which in the sight of God is of great price."*

Questions for Reflection: Wives, do you ever treat your husband with dishonor and disrespect? Do you often point out his weaknesses and faults? Do you patiently forgive and treat him kindly in spite of his shortcomings? Do you ignore his needs and desires? Have you grown careless with your health and appearance? Do you have a rebellious spirit toward him? Have you done all you can do to bring your attitude in line with the pattern God has set for you in Scripture? Is your attitude one of thanksgiving and love or complaining and anger?

The greatest way to see God change your husband is to bring *yourself* under God's pattern for a godly wife. Wives, don't give up on your husband or yourself. Don't make excuses by saying,

"I just don't have a gentle and quiet personality." If you honestly surrender to God's pattern, you will see a miracle in your home!

God's special words to parents - Matthew 18:6 - *"But whoso shall offend one of these little ones which believe in me, it were better for him that a millstone were hanged about his neck, and that he were drowned in the depth of the sea."*

Because children are incredibly perceptive, they usually pick up more from what parents *do* than what they *say*. Often without even realizing it, parents are modeling values and habits that have tragic effects on their children's development. Training up a child in the way he should go is more about daily example than occasionally sharing religious words.

Questions for Reflection: Parent, do you model excitement and joy about worshiping God? Do you consistently express love for Christ's Church or a negative complaining attitude? If your children are expressing a negative attitude toward God and His church, you may need to take a serious look at the attitudes you actually model before them.

Parents, do you lovingly and consistently communicate with each other? Do you consistently take time to talk to your children? Do you really listen when your children talk to you? Do you respond with love and understanding or quickly become angry? If your children are pulling away from you, ask God to reveal ways you may have caused it.

Parent, do you model moral purity by the things you talk about? Have you demonstrated holiness by the things you watch or read? Have you consistently communicated God's standards concerning sex and marriage to your children? Do you communicate in a way that reveals understanding about their temptations and struggles? Have you been approachable and loving? If your children are moving towards immorality, ask God if there are ways you should examine your example. If they won't talk to you, ask God if you've contributed to the barrier.

Parent, do you consistently model honesty and respect for others? Do you break speed laws or cheat on taxes? Have you demonstrated the ability to readily admit your own sins and failures? Do you readily admit your sins or do you make excuses? If your children are demonstrating tendencies toward cheating or lying, you should seriously examine your own example.

Parents, by no means do I suggest that children's problems are automatically a result of parental failure. In fact, Satan often heaps false guilt on parents. However, as parents we must face the awesome power of our example. May God give us the honesty to fully confess ways we have harmed our children by attitude and example.

In many cases, parents will need to ask forgiveness of their children (even older or adult children). Such loving honesty will have an enormous healing effect on strained parent-child relationships. Some of the above questions were drawn by permission from "A Christian Parent's Checklist" by Shelia Jones (E-mail address SJonesAZ@aol.com)

God's special words to children and youth - Ephesians 6:1-3 - *"Children, obey your parents in the Lord: for this is right. Honor your father and mother; which is the first commandment with promise; that it may be well with you and that you may live long on the earth."*

Old Testament law pronounced severe punishment on children who cursed or dishonored a parent. Modern children must relearn the extreme importance of honoring their parents. Today's foolish and wicked society has completely reversed the principle of honoring one's parents.

Questions for Reflection: Children or teenagers, do you disobey your parents? Do you often ignore their guidance? Have you treated your parents with disrespect or anger? Disrespect toward parents is a very serious sin before God. Young people, you cannot be right with God if you consistently disrespect your parents.

As adults, we too must ask whether we are honoring our elderly parents. Do you neglect to call and visit your aged parents? Do you neglect your Mother and Father by failing to give them consistent time and attention? Are you neglecting them emotionally or financially? Do you fail to help them with needs around their home? Are there unresolved harsh words or feelings between you and your parents? Have you truly sought to make it right? Remember, no one who mistreats or neglects a parent can be fully right with God!

Personal Reflection
Sins of Relationships

1. Go back and review the specific Scriptures through which God brought conviction. What relationships need to change? What changes are you prepared to make? List the specific needs below.

2. How do relationship sins affect your walk with God? How do they affect your family? Your church? Be specific.

3. What Scriptures can you claim to find God's victory? List some below.

4. What specific changes are you prepared to make in your relationships? List the first steps below.

Fifth Category
Sins of Commission

Transgression is any act of breaking God's law or doing something God forbids. These sins are also known as "sins of commission." The following Scriptures describe common areas of transgression. Prayerfully consider each one.

Ephesians 5:5 - *"For this you know, that no whoremonger, or unclean person, or covetous man, who is an idolater, hath any inheritance in the kingdom of Christ."*

Ephesians 5:12 - *"For it is a shame even to speak of those things which are done of them in secret."*

Questions for Reflection: Have you committed any form of sexual immorality, uncleanness or perversion? Do you ever watch television or movies that feature immorality and violence? Do you make excuses by saying "There's nothing else to watch"? Do you dress in ways designed to incite lust in the opposite sex? Are you in the habit of reading things that are suggestive or unclean? Do you watch today's filthy talk shows that regularly joke about immorality and perversion? Do you fund Hollywood's poison by going to questionable movies or purchasing videos?

According to Scripture, no one who does these things can be truly right with God. Our society is utterly depraved and many believers have become conditioned to accept pure filth as *entertainment.* God is infinitely holy. If you would know His glorious power and blessing, you *must* reject sinful movies, magazines and entertainment. We should realize that much prime time programming would have been considered R-rated just a few years ago. Yet, God's standards have not changed at all! (And neither should ours.)

---

1 Corinthians 3:16-17 - *"Know you not that you are the temple of God, and that the Spirit of God dwelleth in you? If any*

man defiles the temple of God, him shall God destroy; for the
temple of God is holy, which temple you are."

Our body is the temple of the Holy Spirit and is to be spiritually holy and physically fit for use in God's kingdom. We are to
exercise self-control over our fleshly appetites. In many ways,
overeating and unhealthy diets are as much a sin as smoking and
drinking. We are especially to avoid any form of sexual immorality. If God convicts you, confess this sin and do not rationalize or
make excuses.

God will greatly bless your efforts to give him a healthy, holy
vessel fit for His holy purposes. (*God-led fasting is clearly biblical and very useful as a spiritual discipline.*) For many believers,
regular fasting will also help break the sinful grip of excessive
eating. When we obey God's spiritual and physical laws, we save
ourselves from many of the spiritual, emotional and physical problems that cause pain for so many.

Questions for Reflection: Have you abused your body
through any form of immorality or excess? Do you sin against
God's temple by harmful habits such as alcohol, smoking or overeating? Is any form of drug abuse a part of your life? Have you
been so enslaved to food that fasting is something you make excuses to avoid?

Exodus 20:2-3 - "*I am the Lord thy God, thou shall have no
other gods before me.*"

Matthew 7:24 - "*No man can serve two masters: for either he
will hate the one, and love the other; or else he will hold to
the one, and despise the other. You cannot serve God and
money.*"

Though today most people do not bow to some carved image, we very commonly commit the sin of idolatry. (An idol is
anything we place ahead of God and His service.)

Questions for Reflection: Have you transgressed God's first commandment by placing other things ahead of God? Have other things or people crowded out your worship and service to God? Do you worship and serve God only if everything else is done first? Has your work and financial gain actually become your god? Have you voted for politicians who promote ungodly principles just because they're in your political party? If so, you have definitely placed human politics over God and Scripture. Such practice amounts to plain idolatry.

Do you spend far more time on the Internet or watching television than in Bible reading and prayer? Have you placed your family ahead of God? (*The best way to lose a family is to place them ahead of God.*) Does recreation or some hobby take precedence over God's service? If all church members followed your example of service, how strong would be the ministry of your church? Would there be a Sunday or Wednesday evening service if everyone attended like you? Would there be an outreach or prayer ministry? Who or what is *really* number one in your life? Confess and forsake ways you have allowed other things to come before God. Believe Him to give you a genuine heart of worship.

Malachi 3:8-10 - "*Will a man rob God? Yet you have robbed me. But you say, wherein have we robbed thee? In tithes and offerings. You are cursed with a curse: for you have robbed me, even this whole nation. Bring you all the tithes into the storehouse, that there may be meat in mine house, and prove me now herewith, saith the Lord of hosts, if I will not open you the windows of heaven, and pour you out a blessing, that there shall not be room enough to receive it.*"

God has commanded *all* His children to give tithes and offerings. Failure to tithe is called robbery and spiritual idolatry. Because of this blatant financial disobedience, many believers are not filled with the Holy Spirit and forfeit so much of God's blessing. To refuse to tithe is to place money and things ahead of God. Failing to tithe is nothing less than common thievery against the God who has given everything for us.

It is disturbing that many think nothing of giving a fifteen percent tip to a restaurant waiter, yet find ten percent too much for the Giver of all life. (What does this say about our priorities?) Most would not dare defraud the IRS, yet think nothing of defrauding God every week in His own house of worship. (What does this say about our fear and reverence of God?)

Questions for Reflection: Have you been honest to fully tithe your time and talents to God? Have you been honest in calculating your tithe or have you tithed from the leftovers rather than the first fruits of your income? (Do you give God what's left over after everyone else gets theirs?)

Jesus Christ cannot be Lord of your life if He is not Lord of your finances. Have you figured the tithe to the penny but been stingy with any offerings beyond the tithe? Would you be willing to give far more than a tithe if God leads you? After all, a tithe is the bare minimum God *requires*. How can we not joyfully give far more than the bare minimum?

Spirit-filled believers give cheerfully, generously and sacrificially. Carnal believers put money and things ahead of God. If you sense God's conviction about finances, obey Him now. Friend, you will quickly discover you cannot outgive God! He will give back to you far more than you could ever give to Him (Luke 6:38).

Proverbs 13:11 - *"Wealth gotten by vanity shall be diminished: but he that gathers by labor shall increase."*

God's Word gives clear principles concerning the believers' use of money. In Proverbs, we see God honors hard work and consistent savings. Believers are to do honest work and make wise, steady investments. In plain terms, this means gambling is utterly contrary to God's will! We are to trust God, not chance. Gambling and get rich quick schemes are the exact opposite of God's laws of finance.

America is experiencing an unprecedented explosion of gambling.[9] Through technology, society is becoming ever more saturated with new forms of this spiritual disease. Increasingly, politicians are so ready to put money ahead of what is biblical and right. Mark this well, no Christian should have anything to do with gambling!

Questions for Reflection: If gambling is a good personal investment, why are the casinos getting rich? If gambling is a healthy practice, why do countless thousands become addicted to it? If gambling is good, why do bankruptcies explode in cities where gaming takes root?[10] Have you been deceived into thinking gambling is just a harmless recreational activity? Remember friend, your money is not your own, it is God's. If you have engaged in any form of gambling, immediately confess and forsake this serious misuse of God's money.

Leviticus 19:31 - *"Regard not them that have familiar spirits, neither seek after wizards, to be defiled by them: I am the Lord your God. "*

The Bible leaves no doubt that God hates the use of witchcraft, astrology or spiritual mediums (psychics). Yet today, we have witnessed a worldwide explosion of just such wickedness.[11] In recent years, the world has seen an unprecedented rise in astrologers and psychic mediums. Much of this activity goes under the general term "new ageism." Though it is called *new*, there is nothing new about it. It's simply the age-old practices of the occult.[12]

Tragically, some believers have begun to dabble in what they consider harmless fun or self-improvement. New Ageism promotes the deification of man and many self-help books contain significant elements of such philosophy. For the believer, such practices are nothing less than spiritual adultery.

When we consult the stars or psychics for guidance, we reject God's guidance and open ourselves to the direct influence of Satan. God has given a very clear pattern for receiving His guidance. That pattern is to seek God's face through personal Bible study and prayer. Put simply, no believer should have *anything* to do with astrology, crystals, psychics or any other form of new age practice! (Parents, we must also guard our children from cartoons that are now rife with occultic, new age influence.)

Questions for Reflection: Do you ever consult horoscopes, psychics or any other form of occultic guidance? Have you allowed new age philosophy to slip into your mind by reading self-help books that exalt self rather than Christ? Do you read materials that promote self-exaltation rather than humble surrender to Jesus Christ? Do you have books in your home that promote humanism or new age philosophy? Do you allow your children to watch programs that promote new age ideas?

If God convicts you of any occultic, new age or humanistic involvement, confess and renounce these serious sins. Take specific steps to get these influences out of your home and heart. To do anything less is to open the door to Satanic attack upon your entire household.

Revelation 2:14-15 - *"But I have a few things against thee, because thou hast there them that hold the doctrine of Balaam, who taught Balac to cast a stumbling block before the children of Israel, to eat things sacrificed to idols, and to commit fornication. So hast thou also them that hold the doctrine of the Nicolaitanes which thing I hate."*

The context of this passage is that of Christians who *compromise* their beliefs. In our increasingly godless society, both churches and individuals will face growing pressure to compromise with evil. (And sadly, far too many are giving in.) To be "politically correct," many churches and Christians have already condoned lifestyles the Bible emphatically calls evil. The Spirit of God can never be free to work in believers or churches that are willing to compromise God's truth.

In Scripture, God is very clear about standards of right and wrong. To compromise God's truth means you put the opinions of men over God. It proves you fear men rather than God. In essence, compromise is just another form of spiritual idolatry.

Especially in coming days, believers will be put to severe tests by an ever more perverse society. Yet, this very testing may actually be one of the best things that could happen to us. We should never pray for revival just so we can avoid suffering. Our greatest goal should be holiness, not temporary happiness.

Questions for Reflection: Are you prepared to stand for God's truth no matter what the cost? Do you rationalize and make excuses for rejecting biblical standards? When the pressure is on, do you ignore Scripture and go with the crowd? If God convicts you of compromise, please don't make further excuses. Fully confess the sin and believe God for supernatural power to stand strong. There is incredible reward for all who are persecuted for righteousness sake! (Matthew 5:12) Remember, you can never lose when you stand for Christ and you can never win when you go with the godless crowd.

Romans 14:23 - "*And he that doubts is damned if he eat, because he eats not of faith: for whatsoever is not of faith is sin.*"

This passage contains an often ignored spiritual principle. Though we no longer face issues of eating meat sacrificed to idols, we do face a number of issues that can violate conscience. According to Scripture, if you do anything without a firm conviction it is God's perfect will, you are committing sin. Still another way to say it is: "If you're involved in something about which you have a nagging lack of peace, you are in sin." Indeed, a crucial phrase in the great Welsh revival was, "Brother or sister, are there any *controversies* between you and God?"

Frequently, we rationalize and labor to convince ourselves something is all right with God. Yet, if you don't have peace, deep down in your heart, you know you don't! Friend, if you ignore God's still small voice, you cannot walk in the fullness of His Spirit. When you resist God's Spirit, you enthrone your flesh, and begin to operate in your own human strength, rather than Christ's supernatural power. *This is precisely why many believ-*

ers are spiritually tired and lack vibrant joy. No matter how hard you try, you simply cannot live a victorious Christian life on flesh power! (Romans 7:18)

Questions for Reflection: Is there something in your life about which you have to constantly work to convince yourself it's right? Is there something about which you know you don't have peace, yet you still haven't made any changes?

Do you lack perfect peace about the amount of time and energy you are giving to work or recreation? To financial gain? To personal appearance? To the opinions of others? Though these things are not technically wrong, you sense your level of emphasis is wrong.

What is God bringing to your mind right now? In your heart, you know exactly what it is! Come clean with God and stop trying to rationalize His voice away. Please stop trying to convince yourself something is right when you know it isn't. Embrace the cross and die to yourself. Until you do, you cannot know God's full blessing. Yet when you do, you will discover a freedom and victory you never dreamed possible!

Personal Reflection on
Sins of Commission

1. Go back and review the Scriptures through which God brought conviction. What actions or habits do you most need to change? Be specific and list them below.

2. How do these sins affect your relationship with God and others?

3. What Scripture promises can you use to change the sinful patterns?

4. In what ways are you prepared to change your behavior? What specific patterns will replace the ones that are wrong?

Sixth Category
Sins of Omission

A sin often ignored is that of omission. James 4:17 speaks of this condition. *"Therefore to him that knoweth to do good, and doeth it not, to him it is sin."* Prayerfully consider the following sins of omission.

John 15:4-5- *"Abide in me, and I in you. As the branch cannot bear fruit of itself, except it abide in the vine; no more can you, except you abide in me. I am the vine, you are the branches. He that abideth in me, and I in him, the same bringeth forth much fruit; for without me you can do nothing."*

The most crucial way we abide in Jesus is daily Bible study and relational prayer. Mark this well: it is *impossible* to live in the true fullness and power of the Holy Spirit without daily prayer and close connection to God's Word! Neglecting daily time with God completely prevents spiritual cleansing and growth. Tragically, many modern believers have bought into the tragic unbiblical notion that all one needs is a brief two or three minute daily devotion.

Questions for Reflection: Do you spend significant time in daily Bible reading and prayer? (This *must* be more than a two or three minute devotion!) Indeed, how could we expect to experience genuine worship, thorough confession, biblical petitions and serious intercession in only two or three minutes a day? Have you been too "busy" to give God significant time? *Remember, you will never be spiritually stronger than the strength and quality of your personal time with God.* You must be willing to spend significant daily time with God. (At least 30-45 minutes.) Have you neglected to abide in a close relationship with Christ? Confess and forsake the deadly sin of neglecting significant Bible study and prayer. This is the very *heart* of your relationship to Jesus.

Acts 1:8 - *"But you shall receive power, after that the Holy Spirit is come upon you; and you shall be witnesses unto me both in Jerusalem and in all Judea, and in Samaria and unto the uttermost part of the earth."*

Beyond question, God has called *all* His children to be a verbal witnesses in daily life! If we fail to consistently witness, we become responsible for the lost condition of those around us. According to Scripture, their blood is then on our hands (Ezekiel 3:18).

It is definitely not enough to say, "I witness by my life." Neither is it sufficient to say, "Witnessing is just not my spiritual gift." By such a statement, you are actually saying you're not willing to endure even slight discomfort in order to tell others about Jesus. According to 1 Peter 3:15, every believer should be able to clearly present the gospel.

Questions for Reflection: Have you made a prayer list of people you consistently encounter in your daily course of life? (Store clerks, gas station attendants, work mates, classmates, neighbors, etc.) Do you pray for them on a regular basis? Do you seek to show them special kindness? Do you witness to them about Christ? Do you leave gospel tracts in places you frequent? To be ashamed of Christ is a grievous sin against God and *silence* is one of our greatest failures! (Mark 8:38) Every believer should maintain a list of lost people for whom they pray regularly. All believers should pray for and witness to those with whom they have some connection (neighbors, classmates, family, etc.).

Have you failed to enroll in one of today's excellent witness training strategies? Today there is absolutely no excuse for any Christian not be to trained as a witness. If you have thus failed God, confess this serious sin and obey Him by becoming a consistent intercessor and witness. I strongly suggest that you consider the Lighthouse Prayer Ministry for your own home. (Call 1-800-448-8032 NAMB for information or E-mail HOPE @Missionindia.org).

Ephesians 4:8 - *"Wherefore he saith, When he ascended upon high, he led captivity captive, and gave **gifts** to men."*

God has given spiritual gifts to every believer and your gifts are to be used consistently in the body of Christ. God calls every believer to serve Him and abound in His work. It is a sinful *cop-out* to say, "I just don't know my gift." If you seriously ask God, He will certainly reveal your spiritual gift. Today, there are many helpful tools to help you discover your gifts. If you are truly willing to serve Him, there are scores of immediate needs in your church. In Luke 14:8, we see a tragic story of people making excuses about why they couldn't heed God's call.

Questions for Reflection: Do you continually look for ways to serve God or are you content to sit and be served? Do you make excuses why you cannot serve God through your church? Do you refuse to serve unless it is a high profile job? Have you been willing for everyone else to do the work while you remain a spectator and receive the ministry of others? Are you lazy and irresponsible in the jobs you have taken? Have you failed to exercise your gift with all *diligence*?

It is sad but true that twenty percent of church members do eighty percent of the work and giving in churches. *Which percentage are you in?* Though there are certainly times when your abilities may be limited, you must make sure you are not ignoring God's service by making excuses. (Even homebound people can often serve in a prayer ministry.)

Does God convict you of the need to discover and use your spiritual gifts? Have you been spiritually lazy? Do you sense the need to become a productive member of Christ's church? If you confess your sin and obey Christ in service, you will discover a phenomenal new joy!

Romans 6:14 - *"For sin shall not have dominion over you: for you are not under the law, but under grace."*

Hebrews 4:1 - *"Let us therefore fear, lest, a promise being left us of entering into his rest, any of you should seem to come short of it."*

God has promised full victory over the sins and weakness that enslave us. Yet tragically, many believers live year after year in bondage to the same sins and failures. In many cases, these believers really don't *want* to be free!

Questions for Reflection: Have you identified your spiritual strongholds and claimed God's full victory? Have you determined to overcome the sins that keep cropping up or do you *put up* with them? Do you make excuses for sin by calling it a "weakness" or a "personality trait"? Has Satan deceived you to believe you cannot be free? Have you failed to fully resist Satan until you experience complete spiritual victory? Are you too complacent and spiritually lazy to push forward into full victory?

Whether it is anger, fear or a sinful habit, you must *determine* to get rid of it. Immediately confess the sin of unbelief and determine to settle for nothing less than the full victory Christ purchased on the cross (John 8:34). Though it may require a period of spiritual battle, you will experience full victory if you persist in faith!

James 3:1 - *"My brethren, be not many masters, knowing that we shall receive the greater condemnation."*

Pastors, teachers and leaders have been given a huge responsibility before God! Leading God's people is a high and holy calling. Though it is a glorious privilege, it carries with it a stronger possibility of judgement from God. It is especially crucial for preachers and teachers to exercise their calling with all diligence, integrity and personal holiness. Leaders are indeed held to a higher standard before God. *"To whom much is given, much is required"* (Luke 12:48).

As leaders, we are subject to all the typical temptations of laymen and by virtue of our position, we often face battles others do not face. It is especially vital that leaders focus on deep personal cleansing! Otherwise, we can easily fall prey to sins of spiritual arrogance and ambition. In some ways such sins are even more enslaving than the more outward transgressions.

Questions for Pastors and Leaders: Have you grown lax in the exercise of your responsibility in Christian service? Do you preach and teach the whole council of God or focus only in a narrow range? Have you preached boldly against all sin or become timid through fear of men? Are you afraid to preach about controversial issues such as abortion, divorce and homosexuality? Do you diligently study God's Word or have you grown lazy? Are you doing your very best or have you begun to cut corners? Have you harbored any competition or jealousy toward other pastors? Have you harbored any bitterness or resentment toward your church members? Do you resent low pay or lack of appreciation?

Do you consistently practice what you preach and teach? Was there a time you were more dedicated and zealous in your calling than now? Are you steadfast and immoveable or do you tend to be inconsistent? Are you instant "in and out of season" or do you become easily discouraged?

Have you failed to lead your church in aggressive soul winning and missions involvement? Do you fail to serve with diligence because your position is not as glamorous as the position of others? Have you in any way viewed your church as a stepping stone to a "better position"? Are you a true shepherd or are you a hireling?

Preacher or teacher, please be honest with yourself and with God. What hope has the church for revival if it cannot begin in leaders? Since judgement begins at the house of God, it must first begin in church leaders! Ask God's forgiveness and let His holy fire reignite your service. Believe God to help you to stir up the gift that is within you (2 Timothy 1:6).

Jeremiah 29:13 - *"And you shall **seek** me and find me, when you shall search for me with all your heart."*

James 5:16 - *"The effectual **fervent** prayer of a righteous man avails much."*

In the above passages, we see God desires earnest seekers. God does not chase us down to force His revelations down our throats. He speaks most to those who consistently seek Him in fervent prayer and fasting. Throughout Scripture and revival history, fasting is a frequent part of seriously seeking God. (Though it should never be done as a legalistic effort to impress God or people.) It is sad that many modern believers know nothing of seeking God with true fervency. Typically, their seeking is convenient and costs little.

Tragically, many modern saints are so enslaved to food and earthly comforts that the idea of serious prayer and fasting seems extreme and unusual. (Yet it is the clear pattern in Scripture and all of revival history.)

Questions for Reflection: Are you *fervently* seeking God for more of His daily presence and power? Have you failed to embrace deepening levels of prayer and fasting? Do you resist the idea of any type of prayer that is costly or protracted? Since God required fervent prayer and fasting in all past awakenings, why would He made an exception for us? Since virtually everyone mightily used of God has fasted and prayed, why would His will be any different for you? If God convicts you of the need for fervent prayer and biblical fasting, please don't make excuses or ignore His voice. If you will seek God with *all* your heart, you will find Him in ways you could never even imagine!

James 1:23-24 - *"For if any be a hearer of the word, and not a doer, he is like unto a man beholding his natural face in a glass; for he beholds himself, and goes his way and straightway forgets what manner of man he was."*

A common omission is failure to obey God's Word the moment He speaks. I call this the sin of "showcase repentance." We almost make a game out of dissecting Scripture, yet have no intention of actual obedience.

According to Luke, it can even be dangerous to embrace times of cleansing or solemn assembly. *The danger is that you would make a mere "show" of repentance.* When you are exposed to God's searching Word, He holds you doubly responsible for what you have seen. For this reason, the book you are now reading is almost dangerous. (You are now responsible for what you've heard!) The Word of God is not something you can simply *consider;* it is something to be immediately obeyed. The servant that *knows* his master's will and does it not, is counted worthy of greater punishment! (Luke 12:47)

Questions for Reflection: Do you often sense God speaking, yet you tend to delay obedience? You don't actually tell God no, but you put off your obedience. Believers make the tragic mistake of thinking that "considering" obedience is the same thing as obedience.

Do you consistently fail God in the same old ways? Are there specific areas in which you never seem to make any progress? If so, this indicates you do not have godly sorrow or true repentance over that particular sin. It is vital that you confess your sins of *partial* and *delayed* obedience. Ask Christ to fill you with a genuine spirit of repentance. Though we cannot "work up" true repentance, we can claim it by Christ's indwelling presence. If you sincerely ask, God will give you an obedient heart! *"For it is God which worketh in you both to will and to do of his good pleasure"* (Philippians 2:13).

Personal Reflection on
Sins of Omission

1. Go back and review the Scriptures through which God brought conviction. List specific things you need to start doing.

2. How do the sins of omission affect your relationship with God and others?

3. What promises will help you overcome your sins of omission?

4. In what new ways are you prepared to obey God? What specific behavioral changes will replace your sins of omission? What are your first steps of obedience?

Seventh Category
Sins of Self-Rule and Self-Reliance

Of all the categories, this one may require the most discernment and revelation from God. In this section, we consider subtle ways the old nature remains undetected and very much alive in key areas of one's heart. Beyond question, many believers have un-crucified areas of self that seriously hinder the flow of Christ through their life. This is a primary reason many cannot find the victory God has so clearly promised.

Though some of these principles may seem advanced, they actually represent the foundation of walking with Christ. Before proceeding, it will be helpful to define our use of two basic terms.

The Flesh - In this section, I use the term flesh in the same sense as Paul did in Galatians 5:17-20. In this context, flesh denotes our human actions and thoughts when operating apart from the direct control of Christ.

Dying to Self - I refer to Jesus' statement in Matthew 16:24-25. In this context, one must be willing to choose to deny (or die) to his own wishes and completely surrender to Christ.

As God sanctifies you in holiness, He will lead you through an ever-deepening process of death to self and life to Him. If you don't understand the biblical principles of surrender, you may become confused by necessary times of brokenness which God allows. Without even knowing it, you may start resisting the very method by which God brings you into holiness and spiritual power. Ask God for discernment as you consider three crucial principles of victory over sin and self.

Matthew 16:24-25 - *"If any man will come after me, let him deny himself, and take up his cross, and follow me. For whosoever will save his life shall lose it: and whosoever will lose his life for my sake shall find it."*

Romans 6:6 - *"Knowing this, that our old man is crucified with him, that the body of sin might be destroyed, that henceforth we should not serve sin."*

For all believers, there will be many points we must choose God's will and way over our own (Isaiah 55:8). Our flesh and natural desires may clamor for one course of action, yet we know God wills another. Only as you choose to deny self, and by faith obey God, will you know His glorious power. But do not despair! The Christ within gives you the ability to die to self!

When you were saved, you entered into the victory of *His* death and resurrection. Jesus has already secured your complete death to self and your new life of power through Him (Romans 6:6-11). However, if you obey self rather than God, you immediately lose the fullness and power of His Spirit.

So how do you actually "die to self" in your daily life? In plain terms, it means saying **no** to thoughts, attitudes or actions that you know are of the flesh. Other times it will mean saying **yes** to an action or spiritual service your natural flesh would reject. You deny self and receive victory by "trusting" in *His* death and resurrection working through you (Romans 6:3-4). Friend, Jesus has already won the victory and He is in you! But *you* must choose to reject self and let Him reign in your life (Romans 6:12-14). Though He gives you the strength, only *you* can make the moment by moment choices to walk in Him.

By no means do I suggest this is always easy. At times it will be painful to truly die to self and take up your cross. Indeed, a cross is something upon which you "die." Furthermore, self dies hard and you will often be tempted to give in to its pleading for compromise. Yet, the self-life cannot be improved, it must be crucified with Christ. But do not despair! The Christ who lives within you gives you the total ability to die to self. And after every true death to self, there will come a glorious new release of God's presence! So is dying to self really worth it? Yes dear saint, it's worth it a million times over!

But what happens if you pull back and refuse to fully take up your cross? What happens if you refuse to deny self and obey

Christ? In short, you lose your spiritual energy and zeal. Everything spiritual becomes such an effort and temptation is especially difficult to resist. The results of your prayers and ministry become limited and small. You revert to living in "self power" rather than Christ's supernatural might. *This is precisely why so many believers are spiritually tired and lack supernatural power!* At some key point, they faced the cross and pulled back. They compromised with the old nature and now God's power is short-circuited. They now know little about the abundant life and personal relationship with Jesus so clearly promised.

Thank God, there is a cure that works every time! The cure is simple repentance and faith in the Christ who lives within you. By faith, you *can* die to self and let Christ live through you!

Questions for Reflection: Has God told you to do something and yet you've tried to ignore Him? Has God told you to do something you've yet to do? Is God telling you to stop something you're still doing? Is there some point you know you are resisting God's voice? Have you been unwilling to fully lay family, relationships or work on the altar of surrender? Has God asked you to let go of something that's really not an overt sin, but it is a hindrance?

In addition to actual sins, we must be willing to lay aside every *weight* (Hebrews 12:1). There will never be full victory and power until you daily deny yourself and follow Him. Please be honest with God and with yourself. And never forget, glorious blessing awaits all who truly take up their cross and follow Him.

John 12:24 - *"Truly, truly, I say to you, except a grain of wheat fall into the ground and die, it abideth alone: but if it die, it brings forth much fruit."*

Proverbs 17:3 - *"The refining pot is for silver, and the furnace for gold: but the Lord tries the hearts."*

These passages describe the vital principle of spiritual brokenness. When the outer shell of the kernel is broken, the life within comes forth to produce many more kernels. Yet, if the outer shell is never broken, the life within cannot come forth.

This principle is seen in the death and resurrection of Jesus Christ. Though He had no sin, He was willing to be broken, so that God's eternal life could flow to all. Yet, many believers steadfastly resist God's process of breaking their old self life.

In believers, the outer shell represents those things that are of the old nature and self. (I am using the term "self" to refer to subtle thoughts and attitudes that proceed from our sin nature and natural human strengths.) Though the perfect life of Jesus abides within you, the "old casing" of fleshly thoughts will greatly hinder the flow of God through your life. After all, we're still in a fallen body in a fallen world.

So how does God break old self patterns in order to release His life through us? *God's primary method is the conviction and revelation of the Holy Spirit through Scripture.* By the Word and the Holy Spirit, God opens our eyes to the subtle ways self still clings to our being (Hebrews 4:12). Though this conviction can be initially painful, God is doing it to set you free, not to condemn you! When God opens your eyes to uncrucified areas of sin and self, He calls you to immediately confess the sin and fully trust Christ to be your life at that very point. Out of your acknowledged brokenness and surrender will come His miraculous resurrection power!

A second method of breaking is through the circumstances of life. God sometimes allows significant trials to bring you to the end of your natural human strength (2 Corinthians 12:10). You may also be assailed with great temptations that seem far beyond your human ability to bear. When your natural human strengths are broken, you are then forced to far deeper dependence on Christ's life within you. Jesus Himself becomes your very strength and righteousness.

Such breaking brings you to total dependence on the life and power of Christ. Breaking brings an end to the hidden ways you were still leaning on fleshly strengths or human righteousness. Yet tragically, many Christians resist the very breaking that can set them free. So often, we fight God's processes.

Proverbs 17:3 gives crucial insight concerning God's process of breaking and cleansing. The refiner of precious metal *heats* the object until it begins to break apart. Under the refiner's fire, the previously undetected impurities begin to rise to the surface. The heat causes impurities to become fully evident. Only as they come to the surface can they be detected and fully removed. Without the intense heat, the impurities could not have been discovered and removed.

In much the same way, the Lord cleanses and transforms our hearts! God allows trials and temptations to bring heat (*or breaking*) to our lives. Undetected, pockets of sin and self (that were there all along) suddenly surface under intense pressure. We can then count ourselves dead unto those specific sins and believe Christ to replace them with His own life and holiness (Romans 6:6). Without the brokenness, we may never see the subtle ways "self" still clings to our being.

Questions for Reflection: Do you become defensive and run from God's conviction and breaking? Many people avoid times of deep searching and cleansing before God. They had rather "coast" spiritually and assume they need little further breaking. They foolishly feel they have reached such spiritual maturity that they need not worry about deeper cleansing or holiness. The apostle Paul certainly didn't have that attitude (Philippians 3:13-14). Have you settled into a spiritual "coast" zone? Perhaps you really don't want to grow if it calls for any form of discomfort or seeking after God. Do you resent physical or emotional hardships rather than embrace them as opportunities to more fully experience Christ? Have you been wasting your sorrows by not seeking God's lessons within them?

Though God will definitely relieve many of our trials in answer to prayer, there are some He allows to remain. But rest assured, the trials He allows are for a glorious purpose in your life! Paul himself prayed for the removal of a painful trial (2 Corinthians 12:9). Yet because he realized the trial brought him closer to Jesus, Paul *rejoiced* in His God-ordained suffering and weaknesses. Do you rejoice in your sufferings as commanded in James 1:2? Immediately confess any tendency to complain and resist the breaking God allows in your life. Don't run from God's breaking, embrace it! Glorious life that always comes out of breaking that one receives in faith.

As one precaution, let me warn against allowing Satan to deceive you into passively accepting demonic attack as "brokenness" from the Lord. I know that immediately brings the question, "How do you know the difference?" Let me simply say if you spend time in regular prayer, God will give you that discernment. If you ask, you will definitely receive God's wisdom (James 1:5-7).

---

2 Corinthians 12:9-10 - *"And he said to me, My grace is sufficient for you: for my strength is made perfect in weakness. Most gladly therefore will I rather glory in my infirmities, that the power of Christ may rest upon me. Therefore I take pleasure in infirmities, in reproaches, in necessities, in persecutions, in distresses for Christ's sake: for when I am weak, then I am strong."*

Galatians 2:20 - *"I am crucified with Christ: nevertheless I live, yet not I, but Christ lives in me: and the life which I now live in the flesh I live by the faith of the Son of God, who loved me, and gave himself for me."*

These texts reveal the vital spiritual principle of total reliance on Christ's strength rather than human ability. In fact, Paul rejoiced in the things that ended his strength so he would have to totally depend on Christ. After all, God cannot receive what we try to do *for* Him; only what we allow Him to do *through* us. It is crucial to realize our natural strength can easily get in the way of total reliance on His presence.

In modern life, this can be seen in the way we often major on human methods yet minor on fervent prayer and holiness. If we fail to include fervent prayer and deep cleansing with our strategies, we run a high risk of attempting to do spiritual work in human strength. Even highly trained preachers, teachers and witnesses can do nothing without the deep cleansing and filling of the Holy Spirit.

Beyond question, we should thank God for today's exciting preaching, teaching and soul winning strategies. I urge all believers to use these marvelous methods! But we must never assume that methods and training can replace the fundamental requirement of profound daily cleansing and total reliance on Christ's indwelling fullness.

If we attempt God's work without the full cleansing and fullness of the Holy Spirit, we can end up speaking to people's minds more than their hearts. In turn, this produces many converts that are "ours" rather than "God's." Only God's Spirit can produce eternal fruit that remains (John 15:16).

Though the recent generations have been by far the most programmed and highly trained church in history, our baptism ratios have revealed perhaps the worst stagnation in American history. This reveals a great urgency to combine far deeper cleansing and prayerful Christ reliance with every effort and strategy. No matter how polished our methods, they can only be as powerful as we are willing to be cleansed and full of God's Spirit.

It is no accident that virtually all great spiritual awakenings were led by people of fervent prayer and deep attention to holiness. The issue is not so much the strength of our strategies, but the depth of our personal cleansing and prayer. (Though certainly, we need both!)

Questions for Reflection: Have you actually placed greater focus on your training or natural abilities than deep daily cleansing and fullness of the Holy Spirit? Are you often guilty of being prepared mentally but not spiritually? By comparison, does your church put more focus on strategies, methods and programs than fervent prayer and deep repentance? *May God save us from our own strengths!* We must remember the crucial lesson from Gideon in Judges 7:2. Though we certainly need excellent strategies, we must never place more actual emphasis on them than on deep daily cleansing and fervent prayer. From revival history, we clearly see that God will never share His glory with men or programs! (1 Corinthians 1:29)

Personal Reflections on
Sins of Self-Rule and Self-Reliance

1. Go back and review the Scriptures and questions through which God brought conviction. List specific ways you need to die to self and embrace the cross.

2. List specific ways God may be breaking your self-life to bring you to a deeper reliance on Christ. How do you resist that process? What changes do you need to make?

3. What promises can you claim to find full victory?

4. In what new ways are you willing to take up your cross and follow Jesus? Be specific. Are there areas in which you've resisted God's methods of bringing you to brokenness and humility? Be specific. In what new ways can you cooperate with God's process of making you like Jesus? In what ways have you shown more reliance on human goodness and abilities? How do you need to repent? Be specific.

Onward To
Powerful Prayer and
Dynamic Service

Conclusion

If you have been honest and thorough in confessing your sins, then you are ready for God's full cleansing power. Sins that are admitted and forsaken are fully cleansed. It is important to trust in God's promise of forgiveness, not your feelings (1 John 1:9).

Three guidelines are helpful in your confession:

(1) If the sin is against God, confess it to God, and make things right with Him.

(2) If the sin is against another person, confess it to God, and make things right with the other person.

(3) If the sin is against a group, confess it to God, and make it right with the group.

If there is full confession, there will be full cleansing and glorious transformation. As you confess your sins, ask God to fill you with the Holy Spirit. Do not be discouraged if some sins seem difficult to overcome. Some will require a *process* of frequent confession and claiming Christ's fullness. Don't ever give up and don't feel condemned in the process of the battle. If you persist in daily confession and you truly trust God for Christ's indwelling power, you *will* experience complete and total victory. Don't ever say you can't change when God says you can! (Philippians 4:19)

Friend, it is vital that you believe Christ's death and resurrection provides your victory over sin's *power* as well as its *penalty*. According to Romans 6:6, we are to claim Christ's victory over our sins. As we reject the patterns of sin and self, we then trust Christ to fill us with His own power and righteousness. We can then experience the glorious declaration of the apostle Paul in Galatians 2:20: "*I am crucified with Christ: nevertheless I live; yet not I but Christ lives in me.*"

As you experience this continuing process of cleansing and filling, you are ready for a dynamic daily walk with God. Yet, the absolute key is your prayer life. Beyond question, God wants every believer to experience a dynamic prayer life. He wants you to walk in spiritual victory and experience miraculous answers to prayer. God wants you to be able to clearly hear His voice and learn how to be a powerful intercessor. He wants to teach you how to daily worship and walk in His continual guidance. But how do you move into such a balanced, biblical prayer life on a daily basis? What are the practical steps? The following points provide your starting place.

Five Practical Steps to a Powerful Daily Prayer Life

1. Make an absolute commitment to consistently spend significant time alone with God in uninterrupted prayer.

It is essential that you begin to give God *significant* time on a daily basis. Two or three minute devotions are by no means the pattern of Jesus, the early church or anyone mightily used by God. You must reject the modern notion that you can develop a deep prayer life "on the run." (Thirty minutes to an hour is a good suggestion for a vibrant daily prayer life.) Remember, the only way we learn to pray is to "show up for practice." If you will spend significant time alone with Jesus, He will utterly change your life!

Of course, we also embrace the glorious lifestyle of "prayer without ceasing" (1 Thessalonians 5:17). In other words, we learn to live every moment in the immediate awareness of God. Though we must be very committed to closet prayer time, we should never approach it as a legalistic bondage.

2. Approach your prayer time as a relationship with God rather than a required ritual.

True prayer is a relationship! It is not certain formulas or pro- grams, it is a love relationship with your God. *To view your prayer time as anything less is to miss the whole point of prayer.* More than anything else, God wants your love and this means making time to be utterly alone with Him. We need to reflect on the biblical story of Martha and Mary (Luke 10:38-42). Many are so busy serving God that we neglect time alone with Him. This inevitably stunts our growth and short-circuits our power.

When you approach prayer as a relationship, you will also learn to hear God's voice on a daily basis. Not only will you be talking to God, but He will be talking to you! After all, true prayer begins with "listening" to God. *Genuine prayer always begins in the heart and mind of God!* As you learn to listen, you are then sure what you are asking is God's will.

In many ways, learning to *hear* God is the greatest secret of answered prayer! *"And this is the confidence that we have in him, that, if we ask any thing according to his will, we know he hears us: and if we know that he hears us, whatsoever we ask, we know that we have the petitions that we desired of him"* (1 John 5:14-15).

3. Make a commitment to a balanced prayer life by regularly practicing the four different types of prayer.

It is essential that our prayer life be far more than a list of "needs and wants." God wants His children to daily experience great depths of personal praise and worship. Furthermore, we must experience daily cleansing or we cannot maintain the power of the Holy Spirit. He also wants to deepen our petitions and intercession.

Beyond question, a vibrant relationship with Jesus requires a consistent practice of four basic types of prayer: *(1) Praise, thanksgiving and worship, (2) Thorough confession and repentance, (3) Biblical petition and supplication,* and *(4) Intercession.* Clearly, you can only experience all these prayer types if you make significant daily time to be alone with God. (It is impossible to regularly experience all the types of prayer in only a two or three minute devotion.) But believer, do not despair! Through God's grace, you *can* begin to experience all the prayer types on a daily basis.

4. In your daily petitions, focus more on issues of personal character and holiness than on temporal needs.

It is tragic when our personal prayer life consists mainly of health, finances and other earthly issues. After all, God's great priority is to conform you to the image of Christ (Romans 8:29). He is deeply concerned about filling your thoughts and attitudes with His presence and holy power. But you may well ask, "How can I effectively pray for such transformation in my own life?"

A powerful suggestion is to make the nine fruit of the Holy Spirit your daily personal prayer petition (Galatians 5:22). The fruit of the Holy Spirit represent the very character and holiness of God Himself. As you daily ask God to fill you with each fruit, also ask Him to show you how you *don't* reflect that characteristic. When you thus pray the Word of God for your own life, He will miraculously transform every part of your being!

The specific characteristics of the beatitudes provide excellent personal petitions (Matthew 5). God will also lead you to pray other biblical character words on a regular basis. Some examples of character words are: humility, zeal, discernment, wisdom, genuine worship, immovability, boldness, purity, proper motives, revelation, etc. Ask God to help you focus your personal petitions on character, purity and holiness. If you claim such prayers for your own heart, God will revolutionize your life!

5. In your daily intercession, focus more on issues of evangelism and missions than on temporal concerns.

It is tragic that so much intercession is mainly focused on health and other temporal issues. Beyond question, God's great priorities are the evangelization of the world and sweeping revival in the church (Matthew 28:18). If these are God's main priorities, then they should also be the primary focus of our intercession. God does incredible things when we focus our intercession on lost people, missions and revival! Yet, you may be wondering, *"How can I focus my intercession on God's great priorities?"* Listed below are five powerful strategies.

(1) Develop a prayer list of lost people and intercede for them daily.

(2) Develop a prayer list of the key leaders and ministry strategies of your church. Pray for them regularly.

(3) Compile a prayer list of key spiritual and government leaders. Pray for them regularly.

(4) Regularly pray for vital mission strategies of your association, state and denomination. (You can get daily or weekly updates from your state and national denomination.)

(5) Daily intercede for revival and spiritual awakening in your city and nation. In my book, *How to Develop A Powerful Prayer Life*, I list ten biblical prayers to help you intercede for America and the world. (See resource mentioned below.)

Dear friend, please do not feel that a powerful prayer life is out of your reach. If you are willing, God will revolutionize your praying and thus your walk with Him. For practical help, I have written the companion book, *How to Develop a Powerful Prayer Life*. It is designed to walk you step by step into a dynamic personal relationship with Jesus Christ. *How to Develop a Powerful Prayer Life* is designed to work hand in hand with this resource. In a very simple yet thorough way, it takes you into the depths of a personal relationship with Jesus. (You may secure copies at the address below.)

As we conclude this book, you now have a powerful tool for deep daily cleansing and mountain-moving prayer. Don't let anything keep you from walking in full cleansing and dynamic prayer. No matter how weak you have been, you *can* become a powerful, biblical intercessor. If God is for you, who can be against you? And believe me dear Christian, God *is* for you! (Romans 8:31)

Order Information

We have purposely used a nonprofit Christian publisher and printer so we could make quality resources available at a tiny fraction of normal retail prices. Because of volume printing, we also have the capacity to send thousands of copies in a very short time. To order books for your entire congregation please contact me at the address below:

Dr. Gregory R. Frizzell
Georgian Hills Baptist Church
3759 N. Watkins
Memphis, TN 38127
(901) 357-5333 - Church
(901) 357-9286 - Home
E-mail - gfrizzell@earthlink.net

Church and Areawide Conferences
by Gregory R. Frizzell

- Developing a Powerful Prayer Life
- Developing Evangelistic Church Prayer Ministries
- Developing Associational and Statewide Prayer Strategies
- Developing an Historic and Biblical Vision for a Modern Great Awakening
- Church and Citywide Solemn Assemblies
- Biblical Patterns for Spiritual Warfare

**Appendices
Endnotes
Bibliography
Other Resources**

Appendix A
How to Be Certain of Your Salvation

If you have any doubt about your salvation, I have great news for you. God wants to remove all your doubts and give you absolute certainty! God intends *all* believers to have perfect security in their relationship to Him. The following Scriptures prove this beyond question.

*"These things have I written to you that believe on the name of the Son of God; that you may **know** that you have eternal life, and that you may believe on the name of the Son of God"* (1 John 5:13).

*"The Spirit itself bears witness with our spirit, that we **are** the children of God"* (Romans 8:16).

Since God obviously wants His children to have assurance, why do so many doubt? Though there are several causes of doubt, one of the most common is that people have simply never been saved. In fact, it is widely believed that today's Church contains unusually high numbers of lost members.

In the last several decades, it has been frighteningly easy to "join a church" without having a life-changing encounter with Jesus Christ. For this reason, many people now find themselves members of churches, yet have never had a saving encounter with Christ. You may be wondering, "But why is this so prevalent in the modern church?" The following section gives valuable insight.

Why Are There So Many Lost Church Members?
Four Societal Factors

Though I would never claim to have any idea what the percentages may be, we can safely assume lost church members are not at all uncommon. Four factors give strong clues about the prevalence of lost church members.

(1) *Over the last forty years, America has experienced major moral and spiritual decline.*

There is no doubt our society has experienced a shocking moral plunge. It is also true that many churches are affected by societal patterns. Historically, in times of such spiritual decline, strong conviction of sin and reverence for God tend to lessen. Evidence of deep repentance and godly sorrow are less evident than in times of great spiritual awakening. During such times, history reveals a rising number of church members who evidence no life-change whatsoever. (They don't hold true to their professions.)

In 1 John 2:19, we find a likely clue to the reason more than half of America's church members never attend! *"They went out from us; for it they had been of us, they would no doubt have continued with us: but they went out, that they might be made manifest that they were not all of us."*) Though such members may have raised their hand in a meeting or signed a membership card, they manifested no repentance and often cannot be found even six months later.

(2) *Much modern preaching has placed far less emphasis on repentance and surrender to the Lordship of Christ.*

Consequently, many people have treated Christ as cheap "fire-insurance" to keep them out of hell. In such shallow man-centered preaching, God is almost portrayed as man's servant who primarily exists to make us happy and fulfill our desires.

Though perhaps unintentional, many preachers have so emphasized God's love that the message of His awesome holiness is virtually ignored. Many have failed to preach on the full consequences of sin and judgement. Such shallow, unbiblical preaching is very different from that of the early church. It's also very different from every generation that saw a great spiritual awakening. Under such man-centered preaching, it is frighteningly easy for people to join a church without experiencing the strong conviction that produces genuine conversion (2 Corinthians 7:10). In many churches, there is little evidence of anything remotely resembling the deep conviction and godly sorrow that produces genuine repentance and salvation.

(3) *For much of the past century, church membership was the "popular" thing to do.* (Though this has begun to change dramatically over the past twenty years.)

When church membership is the norm, it can be easy for people to join without a deep personal commitment to Christ. In many denominations, people can join churches with little or no thought about a serious relationship with Jesus. Far too often people are not even asked about their relationship with Christ.

(4) *Churches often fail to give effective biblical counseling to those desiring membership.*

In far too many cases, candidates are instantly received on the mere "assumption" they have been born again. For this reason, American churches have many members who joined the church, but never joined Christ. Their names were put on a membership card, but no one ever led them in a personal prayer of repentance and faith.

Considering these four factors, you can see how easily people could join many churches without being saved. As you have read these factors, you may sense it describes some of your own experience. In the following section, I have listed common statements of church members who later came to realize they were lost. At the time of their original decision, most of these dear people had no idea they were making a false profession. Only in retrospect did they realize why they had made an inadequate decision. Prayerfully consider whether any of these statements apply to you.

Common Reasons for
False Professions of Faith

Peer pressure - "Many of my friends were getting saved, so I did it mainly to be part of the group."

Expectations of Others - "My family and friends wanted me to get saved, so I joined mainly to please them."

Social Reasons - "Many of my friends were members of the church, so I joined in order to belong to the group."

Inadequate Understanding - "When I made my decision, I didn't really understand the gospel. I didn't fully comprehend my total dependence on Christ's blood and His free gift of salvation." (I think I was still trying to "earn" God's acceptance.)

Insincere Commitment - "When I made a decision, I had no real sense of conviction or repentance. Though I made a surface decision, there was no change of ownership in my life."

Shallow, Man-centered Preaching - "For the most part, I heard preaching that was shallow and un-evangelistic. The full gospel of Christ was not made clear to me and I joined just because I thought I should."

Inadequate Decision Counseling - "I did not receive clear biblical counseling when I made my decision. No one led me in prayer for a life-changing encounter with Christ. Though I joined the church, I was never led to pray a prayer of surrender and personal faith in Jesus."

From the above statements, it is clear that people join churches for many reasons besides being born again. So how can you tell if *your* decision was genuine? It really isn't that difficult because the Bible contains clear indicators of true salvation.

Under the next heading, we will examine some biblical signs of true salvation. However, for balance, let me state that even true Christians have some days when all the signs are not so evident. Saved people will occasionally experience times when God seems distant. It is certainly not my purpose to try and scare Christians into believing they are lost. At the same time, you must take these biblical indicators very seriously. *According to God's Word, the following factors will be real and present in the lives of all who are truly saved.* Ask God to give you discernment as you prayerfully examine your life in light of His holy Word.

Biblical Indicators of Salvation

1. Genuine Christians testify to a real and personal relationship with Christ. *"And this is life eternal that they might know thee the only true God, and Jesus Christ whom thou hast sent"* (John 17:3). True salvation is far more than mentally believing facts "about" God. It is actually "knowing" God in a life-changing personal relationship. Tragically many people will miss heaven by about eighteen inches. (The distance between head and heart knowledge.)

2. Saved people have experienced genuine conviction of sin and trust Christ alone for eternal life. *"And when he is come, he will reprove the world of sin and of righteousness, and of judgment"* (John 16:8). *"For by grace are you saved through faith; and that not of yourselves: it is the gift of God"* (Ephesians 2:8).

    No one is saved by intellect. Neither can anyone be saved by just being in church or around Christian people. No one is saved by being a good person. You must be personally convicted of sin and drawn to Christ by the Holy Spirit. There must be a time when you personally prayed and trusted Christ as your own Lord and Savior. Saved persons can readily testify to this reality in their lives.

3. Genuine Christians possess a supernatural assurance they are saved and forgiven of their sins. *"The Spirit itself bears witness with our spirit, that we are the children of God"* (Romans 8:16). This does not mean you never have any doubt, but it does mean a prevailing peace will overshadow any momentary doubts.

4. Children of God exhibit a hunger for spiritual growth and a strong desire to turn from sin. *"And every man that hath this hope in him purifies himself, even as he is pure"* (1 John 3:3). *"Whosoever is born of God does not commit sin; for his seed remains in him; and he cannot sin, because he is born of God"* (1 John 3:9).

   The Bible describes salvation as a life-changing experience. In the physical realm, if something is alive, it has hunger and it grows. Put simply, if someone can consistently live in sin without deep sorrow and God's chastisement, they are not saved. When saved people embrace a willful sin, they are utterly miserable.

5. Genuine Christians sense God's presence and hear His voice in their life. *"My sheep hear my voice and I know them, and they follow me"* (John 10:27). Because salvation is a personal relationship, true believers regularly experience the voice of Christ in their life. Friend, if God never speaks to your heart, you have reason for deep concern. If you have no desire for prayer and the Bible makes little sense to you, it is very possible you don't know the Savior.

6. True Christians have a love for the church and the people of God. *"We know that we have passed from death unto life, because we love the brethren. He that loves not his brother abides in death"* (1 John 3:14). Perhaps the greatest mark of a saved person is a loving compassionate spirit. If you consistently lack any desire to worship and be with God's people, there is strong reason to question your salvation (1 John 2:19).

7. Most saved people can describe a "before and after" in terms

of their salvation. *"If any man be in Christ, he is a new creature: old things are passed away; behold, all things are become new"* (2 Corinthians 5:17). In the case of young children, the sense of life transformation may not be as pronounced, although some changes should be apparent. To be born again is the most powerful transformation in human experience. Put simply, it is very doubtful that old things could pass way and all things become new and you not know it!

After reading the biblical indicators of salvation, you may sense that you have been saved, but at times still struggle with nagging doubts. Are there other sources of doubt besides being lost? The answer is yes. Under the next heading, I briefly describe three possible sources of doubt. We will address them one at a time.

Three Possible Sources of Doubt

If you are experiencing doubts about your salvation, there are at least three possible sources.

(1) *You may have been truly saved, but have since grown cold and backslidden.* It's possible you were never discipled or taught how to walk daily in the power of God's Spirit. As a result, you may have experienced little spiritual growth and are living in a perpetual state of quenching God's Spirit. If God's Spirit is quenched and grieved in your life, you will certainly lack the fullness of His Spirit and often the feeling of His presence. It is possible you are saved, but in need of the cleansing and filling work of the Holy Spirit. If that is your case, working through this resource will produce a glorious remedy for your doubts.

(2) *You may be saved, but Satan is constantly accusing and creating doubt* (Revelation 12:10). If Satan can keep you in doubt, your spiritual growth will be stunted and your service to Christ limited. You may be saved, but simply need to learn how to stand on God's promise and effectively resist the enemy. Our spiritual warfare is definitely real! In later paragraphs, I will give you an

effective strategy for overcoming this type of spiritual oppression.

(3) *You may indeed be one of thousands of lost church members who made a profession that wasn't real.* In most cases, this was wholly unintentional. You certainly didn't mean to make a false profession but for a variety of reasons, you sense you have. Recently, I have seen several deacons, teachers and even pastors come to this realization and get saved. In every case, they came to glorious assurance and a changed life. My friend, you can too!

So How Can I Find Perfect Assurance?

I ask you to set aside the next several moments and get utterly quiet before God. Claim God's wonderful promise from James 4:8. *"Draw near to God, and he will draw near to you. Cleanse your hands, you sinners; and purify your hearts, you double minded."*

As you now draw near, purposely center your thoughts on God, who is certainly with you this very moment. Reflect on the glorious reality that God wants you to be saved and certain even more than you do.

You now need God's wisdom concerning the source of your doubts. You need to *know* for certain where you stand with Him. Pause in prayer and claim the following promise for wisdom. *"If any of you lack wisdom, let him ask of God, that giveth to all men liberally, and upbraideth not; and it **shall** be given him"* (James 1:5).

Now go back and prayerfully read the seven indicators of true salvation. If in the depths of your heart you sense you have been saved but have merely lost God's fullness, then thank Him for your salvation. You should then return to page one and work through all the Scriptures in this resource. As you confess your sins and claim God's filling, you will rediscover the joy of your salvation. Your doubts will melt as you are filled with God's Spirit! (I also suggest that you read "The Illustration of the Wooden Stake" on page 99.)

If in the depths of your heart, you sense you were never truly saved, then thank God for the fact He has opened your eyes. It is certainly no accident you are reading this chapter. God has spoken to you for one reason so that you can be saved right now! It's time for all your doubts to leave.

My friend, you will find peace when you learn to trust God's infallible Word and not your own feelings. Your salvation does not depend on your feelings, but on Christ's unfailing power. Because your salvation is based on God's own Word, carefully read the following Scriptures.

1. **God loves you and wants you to be saved.** John 3:16 - *"For God so loved the world, He gave his only begotten son, that whosoever believeth in Him should not perish but have eternal life."* Dear reader, place your name in that verse. Put your name in the place of the words *world* and *whosoever*. Now I want you to read that verse with your name in it. Read it slowly with your name in it. Read it out loud at least three times.

2. **God Himself is giving your desire to come to Jesus.** John 6:44(a) - *"No man can come to me, except the Father which hath sent me draw him."* The very fact that you are reading this book and have a deep desire to know Christ is clear proof that God is drawing you to Jesus. If you truly desire to be saved, you can rest assured God gave you that desire and He will receive you!

3. **Jesus receives all who sincerely call on Him.** John 6:37 - *"All that the Father gives me shall come to me; and him that comes to me I will in no wise cast out."* Please hear the certainty in Jesus' promise to receive you right now. In essence, He is saying "There is no way I will turn away anyone who sincerely comes to me." By His own infallible promise, Jesus promises to answer your prayer for salvation.

4. **You must receive eternal life as a free gift of God's grace.** Romans 6:23 - *"For the wages of sin is death; but the gift of God is eternal life through Jesus Christ our Lord."*

Ephesians 2:8 - "*For by grace are you saved through faith; and that not of yourselves: it is the gift of God.*" Salvation is a gift that we could never earn or deserve. We receive eternal life by simple child-like faith, not through human efforts to be good. "All our righteousness are as filthy rags" (Isaiah 64:6).

5. **Jesus took all your guilt and paid your penalty.** Isaiah 53:6- "*All we like sheep have gone astray: we have turned every one to his own way; and the Lord has laid on him the iniquity of us all*" and Romans 5:8 - "*But God commendeth his love toward us, in that, while we were yet sinners, Christ died for us.*" My friend, God took all your sins and placed them on Jesus. He took the full penalty and death for all your sins (past, present and future). If you receive Jesus' forgiveness, there is absolutely nothing left for which God could condemn you!

6. **God will give you a new heart and the grace to change.** 2 Corinthians 5:17 - "*Therefore if any man be in Christ, he is a new creature: old things are passed away; behold, all things are become new.*" You don't have to wonder, "Can I change?" It is God that changes you, not you that changes yourself.

7. **You must be willing to repent of sin and to surrender your life to Jesus.** Luke 13:3 - "*I tell you, no; but, except you repent, you shall all likewise perish.*" I want to stress that repentance is not some human effort that *earns* salvation; for we are saved by grace through faith alone. Salvation is all of grace and none of works (Romans 9:11). However, when you have saving faith, it means you recognize the Lordship of Jesus and are willing to surrender to His direction. You are willing (in reliance on His help) to transfer your life to His ownership.

This doesn't mean you will somehow become perfect and never sin again, but it does mean a deep willingness to turn from known sin and follow Him. Salvation is a deep commitment of your life to Jesus, not some cheap ticket to heaven and a license to sin. But friend, no matter how weak you may feel, if you come to Jesus you will receive the grace to change! (John 1:12 - *"But as many as received him, to them gave he power to become the sons of God, even to them that believe on his name."*) When you receive Jesus, you get the power to change!

If you believe the seven things stated above, please read the following sentences and place a check beside each statement.

❐ I believe Jesus Christ is the only begotten Son of God and died for the sins of the world.

❐ I believe God loves me and gave His Son to prove it.

❐ I believe Jesus took all my sins on Himself and died a sacrificial death to remove my guilt.

❐ I believe if I ask Jesus to forgive me and save me, He will answer my prayer.

❐ I believe God's Spirit has opened my eyes and is drawing me to come to true salvation.

❐ By God's enabling grace, I am now willing to turn from my sins and surrender to Christ's Lordship.

❐ I am willing right now to trust Jesus as my personal Lord and Savior.

Dear friend, if you checked off all the above statements, then nothing in heaven and earth can keep you from being saved right now. I'm going to ask you to pray the following prayer. I encourage you to pause after each sentence and let it sink in. You may even want to repeat a sentence to emphasize your sincerity. From your heart, tell God these or similar words. And remember, He *will* hear your prayer!

"God, I know I am a sinner and deserve eternal death and hell. I know I can do nothing to save myself. But I believe You love me and gave Your Son to save me. I am sorry for my sins. By Your grace and help I now turn from all my sins. Jesus, please forgive me and come into my heart right now. I trust You to be the Lord and Savior of my life. Both now and forever, I surrender myself to follow You. Help me live for You and serve You every day. Thank You for keeping Your promise. Thank You for forgiving all my sins. Thank You for grace to turn from my sins. Thank You for giving me eternal life. In Jesus mighty name, I pray - Amen"

Date and Time Prayed: _____

Signed:_____

Dear reader, if you sincerely prayed that prayer, on the authority of God's own promise, **God heard you**! (Romans 10:13 - *"For whosoever shall call upon the name of the Lord shall be saved."*) Do not overly concern yourself with what you feel or don't feel. We are saved by faith in *Him*, not faith in our feelings.

I encourage you to sign and date the time you prayed this life-surrendering prayer to God. Your written signature will become a powerful point of faith should Satan whisper doubts in the future. The following illustration will give you a great strategy for overcoming future accusations or doubts.

The Illustration of the Wooden Stake

There was once a believer who kept having doubts about his salvation. The man thought he had been saved but those terrible doubts just wouldn't leave.

One day God gave him an idea that utterly changed his life. He took a big wooden stake and along with his Bible went behind his barn. He opened the Bible to the promises of John 3:16 and Romans 10:13. He then knelt down and prayed a salvation prayer. He told God he was claiming His promise of eternal life. He asked Jesus to be his own Lord and Savior. After this simple heart-felt prayer, he drove the wooden stake deep into the ground with a little of the top left showing.

From that day forward, when he had failures or doubts, he walked right back to that old stake and said these words; *"Right there by that stake, I know I called on the name of the Lord. Because God cannot lie, I know He heard me and I am His child!"* He then would say, *"Satan you're a liar and in Jesus name, I command you to flee!"* It wasn't long until Satan didn't bother to whisper any more doubts about his salvation. The man soon learned to trust God's Word, and not his own feelings or performance. **Dear friend, your prayer and signature on the page above is your "stake" of faith!**

Do you now see the glorious key? We stand in *Jesus'* blood and righteousness, not our own. We trust in *God's* promise, not our feelings or performance. We trust in *God's* mighty grace to save and keep us, not our ability to deserve it. We trust in God's unending faithfulness to us, not our imperfect faithfulness to Him. Do you see it, dear friend? Your security is in a grace that is greater than *all* your sin. So go ahead, child of God, **rest in Him**! And shout it from the housetops; I know I am saved! I am God's child forever!

So What Do I Do Now ?

Jesus said we are to confess Him before men (Mark 8:38). It is vital that you let others know of the decision you just made. Especially I urge you to tell your pastor. I also urge you to go back and re-read Chapter One and then begin to work your way through the confession guide in this resource. By this you will learn to grow and walk in the fullness of the Holy Spirit.

Your pastor will also provide materials to aid in your growth as a new Christian. At this point many ask, *"What about being re-baptized?"* Again, your pastor should give you the primary guidance. However, I share the following simple principle I have found to be helpful. *If you have a strong sense you were not saved when you were previously baptized, then baptism is definitely in order.* It is vital that you not allow pride to keep you from confessing and being baptized. (I have often seen one person's public profession cause many other lost church members to come under conviction and be saved!)

If however, you believe you really were saved earlier and you just prayed to "drive down the stake of assurance," baptism is not necessary. (Though you should share your new assurance with the congregation.) In either case, I strongly urge you to council with your pastor. Now live your life in the beautiful peace that nothing can separate you from Christ (Romans 8:39).

Appendix B
How to Conduct
Churchwide Solemn Assemblies and
Other Revival Emphases

Today, I am greatly encouraged to see rising interest in deep spiritual cleansing and biblical solemn assemblies. Though admittedly, it is a tiny minority that seriously pursues holiness, it is a rapidly growing minority! This is most hopeful because holiness, purity and deep repentance must precede genuine revivals.

Indeed, we can assemble large numbers and pray until we're blue in the face, but without deep repentance, we will not see sweeping revival. *Prayer is only powerful if it proceeds from people with deeply cleansed hearts* (Psalm 66:18; Isaiah 59:1-2; James 5:16). We can continue to develop aggressive evangelistic techniques, but without cleansed Spirit-filled witnesses and intercessors, we will not see the sweeping evangelistic explosions of past centuries.

Yet by God's grace, growing numbers are re-awakening to the absolute essential of deep cleansing and holiness! More and more pastors are saying, "We will no longer schedule revival meetings and then fail to lead our people into thorough spiritual preparation." Still others are saying "We must do more than just embrace highly organized strategies; we must *combine* these efforts with deep cleansing, fervent prayer and repentance." Indeed, a new day is dawning and only God can explain a growing hunger for holiness!

Today among the most common requests I receive are church leaders asking, *"How can we lead our congregation into true repentance and revival? How can we conduct effective emphases of cleansing and solemn assembly?"* In this Appendix, I lay out general plans for five patterns of individual and churchwide cleansing.

In Scripture, we see several biblical variations of solemn assemblies. In the Old Testament, solemn assemblies ranged anywhere from one day to fourteen days in length.[13]

Furthermore, solemn assemblies are times for believers to acknowledge God's righteous judgement upon His people (or the nation). It is a time to acknowledge our desperate need to return to God for His forgiveness, mercy or special direction.[14] Solemn assemblies are not some casual program or fad. They are times to face up to the fact we have offended God and lost His full blessing and protection.

Since solemn assemblies and other cleansing emphases are the clear pattern of Scripture and all great awakenings, why did we think we could abandon them? Yet, indeed we have done just that! Did we actually believe our organizations, programs and strategies could somehow replace God's timeless patterns of deep repentance and cleansing? Whatever we were thinking, the church (and the whole nation) has paid a devastating spiritual and social price. Our nation now stands on the very brink of God's catastrophic judgement. Yet, many hearts are awakening to a new passion for holiness before God.

At this point, I need to give readers a strong word of encouragement. Do not be overwhelmed by what you read in patterns one and two! These first two patterns are the more intense and not every church is ready for such a meeting. However, patterns three, four or five are possibilities for almost any church. So please don't read pattern one and two and give up on cleansing for your church. Though patterns three through five are not full solemn assemblies, your church could be immeasurable impacted by these basic steps of cleansing! Practically any church could embrace patterns three, four and five.

Though this appendix is mostly about solemn assemblies and revival meetings for Christians, this in no way demeans the special call of vocational evangelists. *In fact, many evangelists could actually prepare for crusades by leading the church in a solemn assembly before the campaign even begins.* Indeed, our evangelists could be mightily used to lead many churches in cleansing and solemn assemblies as well as evangelism.

Pattern One
An Evening Solemn Assembly
(With Two Weeks of Individual Preparation)

Though this pattern doesn't technically fit the all-day pattern of some Old Testament assemblies, I think it can still be done in keeping with the biblical principles of deep confession and repentance. In fact, the two weeks of individual preparation add a very deep level of individuals being exposed to Scripture. I outline this process in twelve steps.

1. *Before the solemn assembly is called, the pastor and staff (or deacons) should earnestly pray about whether an assembly is God's will at that time.* I strongly suggest that the staff go through the biblical cleansing guides before they attempt to lead the congregation! If repentance doesn't first start in the leaders, how can they lead God's people into cleansing? Indeed, they can't!

2. *From the time the solemn assembly is first announced until it concludes, church leaders should spend much time praying for the congregation to take it seriously.* Genuine repentance and solemn assemblies can never be programmed! Unless God mightily pours out His Spirit, you will not experience true cleansing and repentance. In fact, it actually offends God if solemn assemblies are conducted as a flippant program or just another promotional effort. (See Isaiah 1:10-15) ***However, don't be overly hesitant to call an assembly***! If you pray for sincerity, God will surely meet you in mercy and power.

3. *The pastor and church leaders should promote at least a two week cleansing period as the top churchwide priority.* Church leaders should start informing the congregation at least a month before the two week cleansing period. During the pre-cleansing, the church should be fully informed of the specific *purpose* and expected results of the emphasis. It is vital to

communicate what is expected of every church member. (You should heavily stress that every member must prayerfully work through the cleansing resource.)

4. *Choose a particular night for the solemn assembly and begin the individual spiritual preparation material at least two weeks prior to the evening assembly.* I have found Saturday or Sunday night to be most effective. My strongest preference is Sunday night.

5. *Distribute a detailed biblical cleansing guide to all active members (youth through adults).* Let parents decide if their older children should receive the material. Some churches even elect to distribute the material to inactive members. (In many cases, God can use the preparation Scriptures to bring inactive members into deep repentance.) In choosing a cleansing guide for your congregation, I encourage you to secure one that is *thorough.* You can either use this resource or check into some of the others listed in the back of the book. In this resource, we have purposely done all our printing through totally nonprofit companies so it can be offered at a price any church can afford.

6. *Strongly urge your people to pray through the entire resource before the solemn assembly.* Heavily promote the solemn assembly by every means. (Letters, newsletters, bulletins, emphasis in all services, etc.) Unless you make this a huge and constant emphasis, your people will not go through the spiritual preparation guide. They must see this is *not* just another program.

7. *Urge people to actively repent of the sins God reveals through the Scriptures in the cleansing guide.* Encourage them to go to people they may have offended and make whatever public confessions God requires. (They do not have to wait for the night of solemn assembly.) Obedience must commence the moment God speaks. Urge the people to be very cautious not to quench the Holy Spirit.

8. *Give special focus to cataloging the corporate sins of the church.* The heart of a biblical solemn assembly is the confession and putting away of corporate sins (as well as individual). I suggest that the pastor and various church leaders prepare a list of corporate sins for confession. A few examples of typical corporate sins are:

   a. Compromise with sin and failing to declare God's full truth - Revelation 2:14-15
   b. Disunity and bickering (lack of fellowship) - 1 Corinthians 1:10
   c. Tolerating immorality in leadership and members - 1 Corinthians 5:1-2
   d. Lack of prayer as a top priority - Matthew 21:13
   e. Lack of evangelism and missions - Matthew 28:19-20
   f. Financial unfaithfulness to God (paltry giving) - Malachi 3:8-10
   g. Pridefulness and competition against other churches - Mark 9:38-41
   h. Failure to care for sick, hurting or elderly members - James 1:27
   i. Lukewarmness and complacency - Revelation 2:4; 3:15

9. *The leaders should be willing to confess and forsake the specific ways they have fallen short.* If the members see that their leaders are serious about renewed obedience, it will have a major impact on the church body. Obviously, leaders should use great wisdom, as some sins would be utterly inappropriate for public sharing.

10. *Encourage people to fast for one meal each day and if possible spend that time going through cleansing and prayer.* Though fasting should not be legalistically required, sincere fasting should be encouraged as a biblical norm. Some members will be led to go on more extensive fasts. Leaders should definitely call their congregations to fasting and must be willing to set the example (Joel 2:12-16).

11. *On the night of the solemn assembly, cancel all other activities and give at least two to four hours to the meeting.* The entire congregation should be strongly urged to attend. For this event, you may want to alter your time schedule to begin at four or five in the afternoon to allow for a more significant, open-ended meeting with God. True solemn assemblies are *not* brief, highly programmed events! Schedule and promote this meeting so that time is *not* an issue. (As God's Spirit moves, I have known such evening meetings to easily go four hours or more.)

12. *Give very prayerful preparation to the format and leadership of the actual event.* I cannot overemphasize the importance of assembly leaders being utterly clean before God. If the pastor is spiritually prepared, it is usually best if he leads the congregation. However, you may also consider having an outside leader conduct the meeting. (Though that is certainly not required.) If you do get an outside leader, be sure to get someone who is genuinely called and experienced to do the solemn assembly.

In the next section, I give general suggestions for conducting an evening assembly. Though there is no detailed pattern set in stone, some basic principles are timeless.

Sample Format for an Evening Solemn Assembly

I want to emphasize there is no magic formula you must follow to the letter. These events should never be so rigidly programmed that you lose sensitivity to God's leading. However, two elements are eternal and God-ordained.

The two main elements are (1) *Significant exposure to strategic Scriptures*, and (2) *Significant time for prayers of confession and repentance*. I suggest that most of the time be used for personal and corporate prayers of repentance.

In early April of 2000, I conducted a Sunday evening solemn assembly for the First Baptist Church in Houston, Texas. The church closely followed many of the steps I outlined for this type of meeting. Because of intense prior preparation and exposure to a detailed cleansing guide, the people of First Baptist were already under a deep sense of conviction before the solemn assembly even began. (Lack of congregational preparation is the major reason some solemn assemblies have limited results.)

The following outline is the general pattern we used at First Baptist Houston. It was truly an awesome experience of cleansing, prayer and repentance. Only God can explain what happened! Please be mindful the following outline is only a general pattern and you should never be rigidly bound to a time frame.

I Biblical Preparation and Worship

5:30-6:00 - Instrumental Prelude of Worship (During this time the congregation was urged to sit in reflective prayer and spiritual preparation for meeting God)

6:00 - Solo - *We Believe*

6:05 - 6:30 - Corporate Prayer - Scriptural Preparation - United Prayer of Agreement *During this period, Dr. Frizzell laid a biblical and historical foundation for the night of cleansing and surrender to God. 2 Chronicles 7:14, Hosea 10:12 and Joel 2:12-14 were primary points of focus. The message was balanced between great urgency and hope in God's mercy and power. * Dr. Frizzell led the congregation in united corporate prayers with specific biblical focus. During the prayers, the congregations either stood holding hands or knelt at the altar.

6:30 - 6:40 - Small Group Prayers of Reverent Praise and Worship (Congregation breaks into small groups.)

6:40 - 6:45 - Corporate Prayer of Reverent Praise and Worship

II Confession, Prayer and Repentance

6:45 - Biblical Preparation for Confession and Cleansing

   *Dr. Frizzell expounded the biblical importance of full cleansing and repentance (Psalm 66:18; Isaiah 59:1-2; James 5:16).

7:00 - Solo - *Broken and Spilled Out*

7:05 - Sharing Scriptures for Cleansing Thoughts and Attitudes

7:15 - Small Group Prayers of Confession and Repentance

7:35 - Corporate Prayers of Confession and Repentance

7:45 - Sharing of Scriptures for Sins of Relationships

8:00 - Small Group and Altar Prayers of Confession and Repentance

8:20 - Corporate Prayers of Confession for Relationship Sins

8:30 - Sharing of Scriptures for Sins of Commission and Omission

8:45 - Small Group Prayers of Confession and Repentance for sins of Commission and Omission

9:05 - Corporate Prayers of Congregational Confession and Repentance

III Worship and Praise for God's Cleansing

9:15 - Sharing Scriptures of Promised Mercy

9:20 - Celebration of His Coming - Solo - *Midnight Cry*

9:25 - Congregational Prayers of Focused Agreement and Recommitment to Obedience

9:35-9:45 - Final Corporate Prayers of Commitment, Repentance and Celebration of Answers. (All standing and some kneeling around the altar)

Though this outline is very general, it gives some idea of the flow and power of such a meeting. Spiritual preparation of leaders and prior congregational preparation are the *crucial* elements to a successful night of cleansing and repentance. I stress again that we were in no way bound to the times mentioned. For far greater details of this and other solemn assembly formats, contact Dr. Frizzell at the address listed in the back of this resource.

Pattern Two
An All-Day Solemn Assembly
(With Two Weeks of Individual Preparation)

This pattern closely follows the twelve steps I outlined for pattern one. The major difference is the solemn assembly is conducted in an all-day time frame. This fits the technical definition of one type of assembly mentioned in the Old Testament (2 Chronicles 7:8-9).

As in all patterns, I urge a significant period of congregational preparation several days before the actual assembly. In an all-day solemn assembly, you will have more time which allows greater flexibility in formatting. In all patterns, I found it extremely helpful to deal with sins by category. In this way, you thoroughly deal with one area before you move on to another. This is far better than jumping from category to category in a disjointed manner. For all-day assemblies, I usually find Saturday to be the best choice.

A Sample Format for
All-Day Solemn Assemblies

Personal Preparation

8:30 a.m. - *Arrival and Silent Preparation*. People are to arrive at 8:30 a.m. and quietly sit in the sanctuary (or wherever the assembly will be held). In this type of prayerful preparation, participants should re-read some of the Scriptures through which God spoke during the prior days of preparation. (They should bring their cleansing guides.) During this time participants will reflect on God's words and pray for the outpouring of His Spirit.

9:00 a.m. - *Congregational Worship and Biblical Preparation*

9:00 - 9:15 a.m. - Pastor reads and briefly expands on the key biblical texts which set the purpose for the day (2 Chronicles 7:14, Hosea 10:12, Joel 2:12-14). The pastor will share the unique purposes for the assembly in that particular congregation. He will set the tone and atmosphere.

9:15 - 9:30 a.m. - Lead the congregation in reverent worship that magnifies the awesome holiness and majesty of God. (Worship staff involved.) The pastor then leads the congregation in a season of small group and corporate prayer for God's presence, conviction, and power throughout the day. People may stand and hold hands or kneel at the altar during this prayer for God's presence.

Category One: "Sins of Attitude and Thought"

9:30 - 10:00 a.m. - Pastor (or appointed leader) brings a strong message from the Scriptures related to particular sins in this category. He may do it in a sermon form or simply read and expound on key sections from the cleansing guide. (This resource is designed for such use.) The purpose is to drive home the seriousness of these individual and corporate sins. Be thorough in addressing many sins of this category.

10:00 - 10:30 a.m. - The pastor asks the congregation to break into small prayer groups and pray for one another at key points God has revealed. This period is for prayers of confession and prayers of repentance related to thoughts and attitudes. (In all categories encourage people to go to others with whom they may have had problems.)

10:30 - 10:45 a.m. - The pastor (and several others) lead in corporate prayers for God's forgiveness and deliverance for corporate (or churchwide) sins of attitude and thought. You may want to ask people to join hands or kneel at the altar during this corporate prayer time.

10:45 - 11:00 a.m. - Water and restroom break. (Strongly urge people to be back before 11:00 a.m. and keep their talking to a minimum.)

Category Two: "Sins of Speech"

11:00 - 11:30 a.m. - Pastor brings strong focus on the particular Scriptures related to sins of speech. He can either use a sermon or expound on several key texts from that category. He seeks to drive home the reality and seriousness of individual and corporate sins of speech.

11:30 - 12:00 noon - Pastor breaks the congregation into small groups to pray for one another at key points God has revealed. This period is for confession and repentance related to sins of speech. (People should be encouraged to get right with one another.)

12:00 - 12:15 p.m. - Pastor and other leaders guide the congregation in corporate prayers of confession and repentance for churchwide sins of speech. (You may want to encourage people to join hands or kneel at the altar during this corporate prayer time.)

12:15 - 1:30 p.m. - Break and Personal Prayer Time. During the break, I suggest you encourage people to fast and spend that time in private reflection or prayer in small groups. Some may want to quietly rest. Certainly fasting is not required and you should have a light snack and juices available. For those who eat, urge them to take only about thirty minutes. Ask them to spend the rest of the time reading over the next category of Scripture or use the time to pray. A day of solemn assembly is to be very different from the average church get-together. Let the spirit of reflection and reverence characterize the noon break as well. This day is not one for jovial interaction at lunch time. (This could hinder those who are using the time to seriously reflect and pray.)

Category Three: "Sins of Relationships"

1:30 - 2:15 p.m. - Pastor or appointed leader brings strong focus on the Scripture in this category of sin. He can use sermon form or strong emphasis from several key texts. He drives home the presence and seriousness of the specific sins of relationship.

2:15 - 2:45 p.m. - The congregation is broken into small groups for intense prayers of confession and repentance. In this session, it is especially important to ask families to pray together. In any case, people should be strongly urged to find and pray with anyone with whom fellowship is broken.

2:45 - 3:00 p.m. - Pastor (and others) pray corporate prayers of confession and repentance for churchwide sins of relationship. The pastor should be prepared to name these sins specifically. I encourage people to stand and join hands and kneel at the altar (or both).

3:00 - 3:15 p.m. - Water and restroom break. (People should be back before 3:15 and limit their talking.)

Category Four: "Sins of Commission"

3:15 - 3:45 p.m. - The pastor or leader brings powerful focus to specific Scriptures that describe various sins of commission. By God's direction, he will choose texts most needed for that congregation.

3:45 - 4:15 p.m. - The congregation breaks into small groups for extended confession and repentance related to sins of commission.

4:15 - 4:30 p.m. - The pastor (and others) lead in corporate prayers of confession and repentance for churchwide sins of commission and transgression. Ask the congregation to participate by standing or by kneeling at the altar.

Category Five: "Sins of Omission"

4:30 - 5:00 p.m. - Pastor (or other leader) brings strong message and focus on various Scriptures in this category. He will target particular texts as God's Spirit directs. The purpose is to reveal the presence of major sins of individual and corporate omission.

5:00 - 5:30 p.m. - Pastor or leader breaks the congregation into small prayer groups for confession and repentance in this area of sin.

5:30 - 5:45 p.m. - Pastor and other leaders corporately pray in confession and repentance at key points of omission. The congregation stands or kneels in participation.

5:45 - 7:00 p.m. - Evening Break and Personal Prayer Time. During the break, people will be encouraged to either continue fasting or consume a light meal. Again this is to be a time of prayerful reflection and discussion of God, not secular matters. This break should also be a time to get alone with God to process what He has done in you and your church. I encourage you to write impressions in your journal during this time.

7:00 - 8:30 p.m. - Intercession and Worship

7:00 - 7:20 p.m. - Begin with testimonies of personal victories that have occurred during the day. (People can share what God has done in their lives.)

7:20 - 7:40 p.m. - Congregational Worship and Appropriate Solos. This should be part of intense praise and worship of the God who forgives and shows mercy. Ask your worship leader and soloists to prepare for a powerful yet reverent period of praise.

7:40 - 8:00 p.m. - United Prayers of Recommitment and Revival. During this period, the pastor should be prepared to lead the people in focused prayers of recommitment to all key areas of purity, ministry and worship. The pastor should itemize the specific areas of repentance and new obedience to replace the sinful patterns. He should then focus prayer on all the areas of new commitment and ministry. The night could then conclude with united prayers for genuine revival to sweep your church and entire nation.

A Word About Music

Spiritual music and worship can play a vital role in such meetings. I strongly urge that you use soft instrumental music to bring the small group prayer times to an end. Well-placed choruses or hymns can also drive home the significance of a particular season of prayer. An occasional solo or group may further drive home what God has said. The guiding principle is for music and worship to stay far away from "performance" or drawing attention from the purpose of deep worship, humility and repentance before God.

Summary

Let me again stress, the above format is just a general pattern. It can and should be altered as God's Spirit directs each congregation. Above all, never become bound to a schedule. If you do use an outline (for those who lead), do not give it to the congregation. You are concerned with meeting God, not watching a clock. Whether you use some or all of the above outline, God will mightily honor your sincerity! We can all take great comfort from God's glorious promise in Jeremiah 29:13 - *"And you shall seek me, and find me, when you shall search for me with all your heart."*

Pattern Three
A Forty Day Call To
Spiritual Cleansing and Renewal

Forty day periods often have very special significance for times of cleansing, preparation and transformation. We see powerful examples in the lives of Moses and Jesus (Exodus 24:18, Matthew 4:2). Actually there are several ways to approach a forty day renewal and such periods can be called for various reasons. If taken seriously, such cleansing times have awesome impact on individual believers and entire congregations! I recommend three basic approaches that can be embraced by *any* church.

Three Practical Strategies for Forty Day Cleansing Periods

(1) *Church leaders encourage individual church members to embrace a forty day process of personal cleansing and renewal.* I have found it works far better and involves more people if church leaders designate a specific period and keep it before the congregation. Though the emphasis will be promoted by the church, participation is up to individual members. This approach is not highly structured and the people would go at their own pace. However, I do encourage leaders to ask their people to make deep individual commitments to the process. In some fashion, you should ask people to *publicly* commit to the process. (Like signing a sheet or coming forward in an altar call of commitment.) The pastor may want to preach about this emphasis and then call for public commitments.

One of the designated purposes for *Returning to Holiness* is just such a forty day journey of personal revival and discipleship. If used for this purpose, church leaders would ask the people to begin on a certain date and end forty days later. If participants are asked to cover about two Scripture reflections each day, they will generally finish about forty days later. (This allows for some days that will be missed due to schedule distractions.)

One way to enhance the emphasis is a brief weekly overview by the pastor. During the morning or evening service, he would highlight key Scriptures for the coming week's material. He would then urge the people to be consistent with their daily times of cleansing. This is a powerful strategy for keeping the cleansing journey before the people. It keeps the congregation involved, reminded and encouraged.

Another way to strengthen the effect is to schedule a weekly testimony by someone who is going through the personal cleansing journey. The weekly testimonies powerfully effect the church, as well as the person sharing.

(2) *Church leaders call a comprehensive congregationwide period of forty day renewal.*

In this approach, the forty day cleansing is heavily promoted as a major churchwide emphasis. Each Sunday the pastor could preach from some of the Scriptures in that week's cleansing category. It is vital to urge all members (youth through adults) to secure a resource book and make a deep commitment to the forty day process. Because this resource is available for such little cost, *any* church could easily afford it for their people. All you would have to do is ask your adult members to give an extra dollar on a given Sunday. That alone would more than cover your entire costs. The depth and consistency of promotion is vital to the effectiveness of this emphasis.

In addition to the weekly testimonies and initial public commitment, I have found that the pastor's sermons will have an awesome impact on congregational cleansing. A powerful strategy is for the pastor to target each week's sermon (or sermons) to the sin category of the previous week's cleansing guide. The forty day emphasis could involve either six or seven Sundays. The scriptural material is designed to thoroughly focus on all seven categories of individual and corporate sin. The uniqueness of this resource is its *thoroughness* in covering all categories of sin and growth. Even beyond a forty day period, many pastors may consider preaching through all the Scriptures contained in the seven categories of sin. (This could be done on Sunday evenings.)

The pastor can use that week's Scriptures to easily develop a wide-range of related sermons. Each pastor would let God guide him for his unique congregation. As individuals are convicted in their personal cleansing process, the pastor then follows with a biblical message on that very issue. The effects are awesome! Such a process also aids the pastor in preaching biblical messages on the *whole range* of potential sin. This emphasis can greatly broaden and intensify the pastor's preaching to all the sins and needs of the church.

(3) *Call for a forty day period of cleansing that precedes scheduled revival meetings or churchwide solemn assemblies.* It is astounding that thousands of churches schedule yearly and bi-yearly revivals with absolutely no prior cleansing or preparation among their people. No wonder most of these "scheduled" revivals seldom become genuine revivals. It is utterly unbiblical to attempt revival efforts or evangelistic crusades without a serious process of biblical cleansing and repentance! If done at all, church cleansing emphases are typically very shallow and incomplete. We tend to gloss over the issue of serious cleansing and repentance. Yet, when intense prayer and cleansing precede major events, God proves He can still shake whole cities!

Serious periods of cleansing and prayer should also precede major church decisions or intensive evangelistic initiatives. You should also consider special cleansing in times of unusual Satanic attack. Cleansing should certainly be done when

God's chastises or withholds His blessing. Friends, when we return to God's changeless patterns of cleansing and repentance, we will again see sweeping floods of nationwide revival and evangelism. Until we do, we won't!

Pattern Four
Revival Meetings That Focus on Cleansing and Repentance

One of the tragic signs of modern times is the Church's departure from the protracted periods of repentance seen in Old Testament revivals and all church age great awakenings.[15] In the modern quest for *convenience*, we have scheduled meetings that are so brief (and biblically shallow) that true revival is virtually impossible. In essence, we have "scheduled" ourselves right out of genuine God-sent revival.

Furthermore, most modern revival meetings are not revivals at all. For the most part, they are brief evangelistic campaigns. Though we desperately need the evangelistic campaigns, these can never replace the desperate need for major times of deep biblical cleansing in the church. Interestingly enough, history proves the greatest thing we could possibly do for evangelism is to lead the church back into serious repentance! When the church experiences true revival, conversions not only explode many fold, they prove to be far more genuine and lasting![15]

So how can you lead your congregation into true cleansing and revival? Certainly there is no magic format, but there are changeless biblical patterns. To summarize again, they are: (1) *Intensive exposure to Scriptures that convict of specific sins* and, (2) *Leading God's people into intense times of protracted prayer and repentance.*

I am fully convinced we *can* return revival meetings to their God-ordained purpose. The following pages reveal practical guidelines for returning to revival meetings that are truly biblical and life-changing.

Practical Steps for
Biblical Revival Meetings

1. *Schedule the meeting far enough in advance to allow for numerous preparatory prayer meetings.* I strongly suggest both

cottage and churchwide prayer meetings weeks in advance. Also, give your people specific biblical guides in how to pray for the revival and cleansing emphasis. (Obviously, nothing will happen without intense, focused prayer.)

2. *Urge all active members to prayerfully work through a comprehensive cleansing guide prior to the actual meeting.* I recommend at least a two week preparation period. You may well want to consider a forty day preparation.

3. *During the preparation period and the revival itself, encourage your people to fast at least one meal each day and spend that time in prayer and biblical cleansing.* (Fasting should never be required or done in a prideful, legalistic manner.) The pastor should give his congregation basic teaching in the various types of fasts. (It is vital that we teach our people the divine purpose of fasting rather than just the mechanics.)

4. *Each night, the pastor (or guest preacher) will preach on one of the seven major categories of sin.* The preaching will be followed by a significant time of small group and corporate prayers of confession and repentance. (See Pattern One and Two for ideas.) A major time of invitation will be offered toward the end of the service. The invitation is the time people will respond with public decisions and commitments. People will be urged to respond publicly to God's dealing in their life. As in other revival meetings, sensitive, God-led music is of great value.

5. *The pastor can use Scriptures in the cleansing guide to direct his sermon, as well as the times of cleansing and repentance.* Each night the preacher would focus on one category of sin. He would deal with the sin in a very focused and biblical manner.

This type of revival meeting is especially powerful for two reasons: (1) The people are involved in deep personal and united preparation. In addition to fervent prayer, they are fully exposed to God's Word in every key area of their lives. (2) The meetings themselves are heavily focused on dealing biblically with the sins and spiritual needs of the church. These are not man-centered topical sermons. The messages go deep into every key area of individual and corporate church life. Issues of sin and self are exposed in a very thorough and comprehensive manner.

Believers, why in the world would we think we can have revival without this type of emphasis? Though such meetings are different from the norm, they are both practical and powerful. By God's grace, we *can* return to the age old patterns of sweeping revival! And beyond question, God is waiting to meet us right where we left Him at the place of thorough repentance and fervent prayer.

Pattern Five
Discipleship Training Prayer Groups Which Focus on Cleansing and Repentance

Today we face an urgent need to return God's people to discipleship that is dynamic and life-changing. Indeed, can there be any real discipleship that doesn't include an intense focus on deep spiritual cleansing and prayer? I believe the answer is no! The very heart of growth is daily exposure to powerful Scriptures that search various areas of our lives. Then our prayers and soul winning will take on mountain-moving power!

Returning to Holiness was purposely arranged in a fashion perfect for small group study and prayer. Indeed, there is a power in small group study and prayer that is hard to equal. ***Prayerfully consider the following steps to revolutionize your discipleship training and prayer groups ministries.***

1. *Promote the cleansing resource as a quarterly discipleship training course for spiritual growth and personal revival.* In this manner, your people will study a comprehensive array of Scriptures which deal with all areas of their lives. Thank God, there is growing interest in the subject of deep cleansing and repentance. This discipleship training course functions in the following manner:

    (a.) Ask a mature Christian to be the leader or facilitator of the group. (He or she will guide the discussion and prayer times each week.) The leader simply uses the Questions for Reflection at the end of each section. Group members are asked to respond to the discussion questions. In the last twenty minutes of the meeting time, the leader guides the members in a time of group prayer for points of confession or needed growth.

(b.) During the week, group participants are expected to study and pray through half of one of the seven categories. (At the weekly meeting, the group will decide where to stop in their reading for the coming week.) If you take half a category each week, you will finish in about 13 weeks. To insure that you finish, you might choose one week to cover a whole section.

However, the discipleship groups should feel the flexibility to move at their own pace. After all, this process is designed as a relationship with God, *not* a rigid program with no variance. In fact, many groups will elect to make this course as a 26 week study. (Especially if their meeting time is only an hour.) I also recommend that study groups be done in homes so you can have an open-ended time frame.

(c.) In the weekly session, each person should be asked to establish specific steps of obedience to what God has revealed. This course is not designed merely for study! It is designed to guide believers in concrete steps of repentance and obedience. The group will help hold each other accountable to follow through with commitments made.

2. *Require this cleansing guide (or some effective guide) for all who work in your church prayer ministry or evangelistic teams.* It should also be a requirement for all deacons and Bible teachers. We must move away from the pattern of an enormous emphasis on methodology and strategies which only *assumes* our leaders are clean before God. In a high number of cases, that is a dangerous and false assumption. May we return to the unshakable truth that our programs and strategies will only be as powerful as the spiritual cleansing and prayer power of those who use them. Everyone who commits to a soul-winning team should be *required* to go through a serious cleansing process at least two weeks before they begin their training! Otherwise, we run a high risk of sending out witnesses who are not thoroughly cleansed or genuinely full of the Holy Spirit.

This cleansing guide is a simple Bible-centered tool that is very flexible by design. Be creative and let God guide you into an ever deepening relationship with Himself.

Conclusion

For far too long we have forgotten that God is indescribably holy. Yet even now, He is calling us back to Himself and to deep repentance. Can we really afford to go on with church business as usual?

Where will America be in just a few years if we see no massive Great Awakening? Surely we are at last beginning to realize our primary answer is not just a better strategy. If new strategies could have brought a sweeping awakening, our generation would have long since seen the biggest revival in the history of the world. Yet, in spite of a fifty year explosion of new programs and strategies, we have seen by far the biggest moral collapse and baptism stagnation in American history.

Friends, it is now time for a new spiritual paradigm. Yet, the paradigm is not new at all. It is the old biblical paradigm that's never changed and never will. It's not that we need less programs. Indeed our programs are excellent and we should always be seeking better ways to do God's work. But we must also return to God's primary path to sweeping revival and explosive evangelism. That way has never changed. *It is a return to deeper repentance and fervent united prayer. Our evangelistic results will then explode many-fold.* I can think of no better way to close this book than with God's own words of invitation. May God help us settle for nothing less than all of Himself!

"Therefore also now, saith the Lord, Turn you even to me with all your heart, and with fasting, and with weeping, and with mourning. And rend your heart, and not your garments, and turn to the Lord your God: for He is gracious and merciful, slow to anger, and of great kindness, and repent Him of the evil. Who knows if He will return and repent, and leave a blessing behind Him." Joel 2:12-14

"Sow to yourselves in righteousness, reap in mercy; break up your fallow ground: for it is time to seek the Lord, till he come and rain righteousness upon you." Hosea 10:12

Endnotes

1. H. Brian Edwards, *Revival! "A People Saturated with God,"* (Durham, England: Evangelical Press, 1990), 112-115.

2. Reports of Vocational Evangelists: anecdotal

3. George Barna, *The Frog in the Kettle*, (Ventura, California: Regal Books, 1990), 117.

4. Ron Blue, *Storm Shelter: Protecting Your Personal Finances*, (Nashville, Tennessee: Thomas Nelson Publishers, 1994), 129.

5. H. Robert Bork, *Slouching Towards Gommorah*, (New York, New York: Harper Collins Publishers, Inc., 1996), 134.

6. Rodney J. Crowell, *Musical Pulpits: Clergy and Lay Persons Face the Issue of Forced Exits*, (Grand Rapids, Michigan: Baker Book House, 1992), 21.

7. G. Lloyd Redeger, *Clergy Killers*, (Louisville, Kentucky: Westminster J Knox Press, 1997), 32.

8. Barna, 133.

9. Larry Braidfoot, *Gambling: "A Deadly Game,"* (Nashville, Tennessee: Broadman Press, 1985), 15.

10. Ibid., 148-149.

11. Karen Hoyt, *The New Age Rage*, (Old Tappan, Jew Jersey: Fleming H. Revell Company, 1987) 17-19.

12. Stephen F. Olford, *Heartcry for Revival*, (Memphis, Tennessee: EMI Books, 1987), 78.

13. Richard Owen Roberts, *Sanctify the Congregation*, (Wheaton, Illinois: International Awakening Press, 1994), 10.

14. Ibid., 3-5.

15. Richard Owen Roberts, *Glory Filled the Land*, (Wheaton, Illinois: International Awakening Press, 1989), 115.